Golden Keys of Gaia
ORACLE OF ELEMENTAL WISDOM

VANESSA TAIT Artwork by HANNAH ADAMASZEK

Golden Keys of Gaia

ORACLE OF ELEMENTAL WISDOM

Copyright © 2024 Vanessa Tait
Artwork © 2024 Hannah Adamaszek

All rights reserved. Other than for personal use, no part of these cards or this book may be reproduced in any way, in whole or part, without the written consent of the copyright holder or publisher. This publication is intended for spiritual and emotional guidance only. The content is not intended to replace medical assistance or treatment. The views and opinions expressed by the author, both within and outside of this publication, do not necessarily reflect the views of the publisher.

Published by Blue Angel Publishing®
10 Trafford Court, Wheelers Hill,
Victoria, Australia 3150

info@blueangelonline.com
www.blueangelonline.com

Edited by Peter Loupelis and Jules Sutherland
Designed by Sunshine Connelly

Blue Angel® is a registered trademark
of Blue Angel Gallery Pty Ltd.

ISBN: 978-1-922574-01-5

Contents

Overview

Acknowledgements — 08

Gaia's Gown — 10

The Gates of Gaia's Realm — 12

Using the *Golden Keys of Gaia* — 18

Card Spreads — 20

Card Messages — 25

Mirror, Mirror on the World — 163

About the Author — 199

About the Artist — 200

The Golden Key of Earth

1. Communication — 27
2. Grounding — 30
3. Patience — 33
4. Patterns — 37
5. Growth — 42
6. Gratitude — 45
7. Wisdom — 49
8. Compassion — 52
9. Give Yourself a Break — 55
10. Abundance — 59

The Golden Key of Air

11. Winds of Change — 64
12. Rainbow Bridge — 67
13. Abracadabra — 70
14. Creative Expression — 73
15. Forgiveness — 76
16. Freedom — 79
17. Inspiration — 82
18. Imagination — 86
19. Magic — 90
20. Transformation — 93

The Golden Key of Fire

21. Flame of Passion — 98
22. Courage — 101
23. Burning Desire — 105
24. Integrity — 108
25. Shine Bright — 112
26. Be Brave — 115
27. Phoenix Rising — 118
28. Rekindle — 121
29. Mask Off — 124
30. Burnout — 128

The Golden Key of Water

31. Listen Closely — 133

32. Detoxify — 136

33. Go with the Flow — 139

34. Heart's Treasure Chest — 142

35. Peace of Mind — 145

36. Reflection Time — 148

37. Release — 151

38. Surrender — 154

39. Unfoldment — 157

40. Voyage of the Heart — 160

The Golden Key of Spirit

41. Beauty — 166

42. Web of Life — 170

43. Ask for Help — 173

44. Altar of Heart — 176

45. Ritual — 179

46. Find Balance — 183

47. Intuition — 186

48. Law of Attraction — 189

49. Divine Love — 192

50. Wish upon a Star — 195

Acknowledgements

First and foremost, I offer my gratitude to Gaia, our precious Earth and guardian of the five elements, whose wisdom has been the guiding light behind this creation. It is a deep honour to serve as a channel for your sacred teachings.

I also thank the numerous past and present teachers, healers, authors, and wisdom keepers whose words have shaped my literary voice and who I am as a person today.

To my incredibly supportive and loving family—my mother, who has been my pillar of strength and endless source of encouragement; and my father, always supporting my dreams and visions, no matter how far-fetched, and my two brothers, my fellow musketeers and partners in both mischief and camaraderie. Being triplets has bonded us in a unique and special way, and I'm grateful for the love and understanding we share as siblings. Your belief in me and my creative endeavours has meant the world, and this journey wouldn't have been the same without you both there by my side.

To my circle of amazing friends, each of you has played a significant role in shaping my path and providing me with the encouragement needed to keep going. A special mention goes to my best friend Silke, whose presence and belief in me have been a constant source of strength. Thank you for being my rock through it all.

And to my literary agent, Bill Gladstone, your guidance and belief in my work have been invaluable. You've helped me navigate the complexities of the publishing world with grace and expertise, and I'm grateful for the opportunity to work with you. Additionally, I extend my gratitude to editors Peter Loupelis and Martin Jeeves, whose keen insights and dedicated efforts brought my vision to life on the pages. Your contributions have made this creative journey an absolute joy.

I want to acknowledge Hannah's artistic talents and collaborative spirit, her illustrations breathed beautiful life into this deck, adding the vital visual dimension. Witnessing thoughts materialise into form has been an absolute delight! Our collaboration has flowed effortlessly and evolved beautifully over the four years of crafting this deck, mirroring the blossoming of a cherished friendship.

My appreciation extends to you, the readers and users of *Golden Keys of Gaia*. May these cards bridge you to the elemental healing energies, leading you towards inner harmony and your true self.

This oracle deck embodies my love and life's work, and I am profoundly privileged to share my heart with yours. May it ignite and nurture a profound connection to the elemental forces within you and this magical natural world that surrounds us.

With gratitude and love,

Vanessa

Gaia's Gown

Gaia's gown dresses the entire landscape,

the fabrication of life flows through the hems of the hemispheres,

sewn tight to the soil and soul of our world.

From the verdant green of the Amazon rainforest,

to the golden plains of the Serengeti,

her garment graces and embraces every edge.

As the wind caresses the folds of her gown,

it carries the fragrance of blooming flowers

that flow through the ruffled meadows,

and dances down desert-dune creases and oceanic pleats alike.

It seems the seams intertwine so subtly with the roots of towering trees,

nurturing life and breathing vitality into the very fabric of existence.

The sun's touch reveals sequined stars, shimmering in celestial strobe,

against her robe reflecting her eternal love to the universe and back,

to the buttons beneath the silk surface,

fastened to the corset core of the earth.

Interlacing molten and mineral materials to make her assets adore

her curves and contours, mountains and mounds

become an embellishment to explore.

And as a final touch, a tiara of lunar light,

a crescent crown, the magnificent moon

delicately rests upon her head.

The Gates of Gaia's Realm

James Lovelock—a British scientist, environmentalist, and futurist—wrote a groundbreaking book on what has famously become known as 'Gaia theory', a concept that opened the gates to a new realm of thought. He proposed the idea that the earth is, in and of itself, a living and divine spirit. Our planet is not simply 'a rock' floating in space, but exists as a self-evolving, self-regulating sentient being, affectionately named Gaia. Gaia has her own cycles, rhythms, and pulse — with which we, and all of life, pulsate and orchestrate in unison to. The natural rhythm of her pulse keeps life continuously flourishing, yet balanced all the same. Even as the sun has moved closer, and our planet has become warmer, she has maintained her temperature over the four billion years she has been alive so far. She has cycled through times of purposeful cooling, when the ice caps swell, reflecting more of the sun's heat away, to also growing warmer, so that the ice caps shrink. Each mass extinction that has ever taken place has acted as sacred initiation, enhancing Earth's sustainability as a habitat and making her womb—our world—a better place to live.

We are born of the earth, and we return to the earth. In the meantime, we assume the noble mantle of gardeners and guardians to this wondrous planet that we share as our home. We are the children of our great Mother Gaia — the creatrix whose magick mirrors all things. All that she birthed into being are our brothers and sisters — from flora to fauna, sentients to sediments. All that exists now and before us came from the same waters of her womb.

The blood of Mother Earth and her veins make up our rivers. Her blood flows, giving life to the animals, plants, mountains, and humanity. Our human bodies are made largely of water, and from the time we are in our mother's womb, we are connected with the water and the cycles of Grandmother Moon, Grandfather Sun's rotation, and the seasonal cycles of our Great Mother.

We are all living through a moving mythology, integrated into a collective universe. The cycles of the stars, the sun, and the moon mark our stories and ground us in the past, create our present, and build our future. The only things that separate us from each other, nature, and the Divine are our own misguided perceptions. We mistakenly see nature—also referred to as 'the outside'—as separate and devoid of soul. Merely a backdrop to a nice walk or picnic, or simply as a landscape to be moved through on our way to somewhere else, or solely a soulless commodity to take from, to use for our benefit. Many of us understand the importance of the natural world from a life-sustaining perspective, but most have forgotten our authentic place here.

But we are nature. Our bodies are made from the earth, we couldn't separate ourselves even if we tried. The salt in our sweat is the same salt that is in the sea; our lungs mirror the same design to the branches of a breathing tree, as does the Tree of Life resemble a human placenta. See how the composition of human veins resemble leaf veins and river networks; tree stumps to human fingerprints. There is an entire inner universe that lies behind the deep, black void of our pupils. We are of earth, water, fire, and air, with our spirits and souls bound by the ethereal realm. When we detach ourselves mentally from this sacred union with the earth, we lose touch with our own essence.

But fear not, for Gaia is guiding us, leading us to the door home to our hearts—the gateway to Eden, the place of heaven embodied—through her echo. She holds the Golden Keys, which are hidden within her elemental realm, allowing us to unlock and enter through the doors of this deep inner discovery. Be willing to open your eyes and heart wider and listen with all your senses to hear her. She only reveals her secrets to those who tune in to her rhythms and walk her healing paths of knowledge. Listen to her in the whispers of the winds, feel her warmth in the flames, sense her embrace as you immerse yourself in the waters. She is there in the ether and below the grounding soils. Feel her cradle and caress you within every step and breath you take.

You must switch your gaze from a linear lens to that of the holistic heart, to see clearly—yet more intricately—a kaleidoscope of colourful cycles and patterns that play off each other in this Earth's dream. This gaze fosters perpetual shifts in perspective, facilitating the growth of your soul and enabling you to experience the inner Eden. Through this new perspective, you can gain a deeper 'inner-standing' of how nature influences us both externally and internally, and how these interactions can lead to either balance or imbalance.

These are the teachings passed down from our ancestors, our wise forebears who revered our planet as the Goddess — the Matriarch, our One Divine Mother. Honouring her as not merely a 'background' but a living, breathing, sentient being with consciousness — a nurturing force that births and sustains all life.

UNLOCKING THE GOLDEN GATES

This deck is a declaration, a voice, a legacy of our ancestors and their powerful wisdom, illuminating the pathway they undertook to discover the *Golden Keys of Gaia*. With each card you draw, prepare not only to receive a potent message for the day, woven with messages and omens from the natural world, but also to delve into the depths of Gaia's treasury of gifts. This oracle goes beyond surface knowledge, offering excerpts of extensive wisdom imparted through the captivating tales, ancient insights, and gentle guidance given within this guidebook.

Immerse yourself in these teachings, allowing them to assist you in the harmonisation of your own inner earth, enabling the expansion of your awareness to reach into higher states of consciousness. Embrace the transformative power to magnetise your grandest visions, manifesting them with divine grace. This deck comes to you as your faithful ally on your journey of self-discovery. On your quest to unlock the golden gate of your heart , you will forage within the corridors and corners of your mind and forge a profound yet intimate connection with yourself, the harmonics of nature, and the *anima mundi* — the world's soul.

Interwoven within each Invitation passage are tangible exercises and practical activities. May these sacred offerings serve as more than momentary aids and become powerful, lifelong tools that integrate into your mental toolkit, ready to assist you in any moment.

Above all, may this deck serve as a gentle reminder that everything on this planet is in partnership and sacredly connected. We are all children of Gaia — our Great Mother Earth is the wild, divine feminine, she is the medicine we all seek, and the re-connection to her is our cure.

THE GOLDEN KEYS

The five elements—earth, air, fire, water, and spirit—serve as keys that unlock profound spiritual truths within us through their natural expressions. Each element represents distinct aspects of our inner being and imparts valuable lessons and insights that contribute to our personal growth and self-awareness.

Earth symbolises stability, grounding, and a sense of security. It encourages us to cultivate resilience, find balance, and embrace the physical aspects of our existence.

Air represents intellect and communication, stimulating our mental faculties and fostering clarity of thought. It encourages us to explore diverse perspectives, engage our imagination, and expand our understanding of the world.

Fire encompasses passion and transformation, igniting our inner power and propelling us to pursue our desires and goals. It nurtures self-confidence, courage, and the willingness to embrace change and personal growth.

Water embodies emotions and intuition, guiding us to delve deep within ourselves and explore our inner world. It teaches us to flow with our feelings, embrace vulnerability, and trust our intuitive wisdom.

Spirit transcends the physical realm, connecting us to the Divine and our higher self. It beckons us to explore our spirituality, seek meaning and purpose, and cultivate a sense of interconnectedness and universal love.

By embracing and engaging with these elemental energies, we unlock dormant parts of our psyche that innately know how to live coherently with these universal forces. The elements serve as mirrors that piece together to form Gaia's grand looking glass, reflecting to us the aspects of our being that require some attention, nurturing, or transformation.

Through introspection and the embodiment of the elements, we gain profound insights into our strengths, limitations, passions, and purpose. Unlocking all five seals leads to a more profound and harmonious life experience. In the context of the alchemical five elements, the maxim 'as above, so below' reflects the alchemist's wisdom, embodying the conscious integration of the spiritual and the material. This maxim recognises the fundamental unity that bridges our inner and outer worlds, acknowledging that the elements encompass not only the composition of the physical realm but also represent aspects of the human psyche and spiritual journey. Furthermore, it acknowledges how our actions in the physical world resonate and influence our inner world, just as our inner thoughts and emotions manifest in the external world.

Thus, we must—first, foremost, and forever—be students of nature, deepening our connection with the natural world to deepen our understanding of ourselves. As above, so below — and behold, in between lies the gateway, from which all keys lead.

We ultimately hope that you find your way to uncover the Mother's master key, which can only be found within you — unlocking the golden gates to your inner Eden in this lifetime, with the realisation that we are already living within the Kingdom of Heaven — Gaia's Queendom, and Earth's dream.

Heaven is not a destination, it is a place of perception.

Using the *Golden Keys of Gaia*

In the world betwixt and between the physical and metaphysical lie answers to non-logical and non-linear questions. Nature herself is a doorway for divination. But for us humans, divination tools such as oracle cards help us communicate with and through her, into other far-out realms, and to entities beyond human conception within our universe. The cards bridge this communion with our guardian angels, the elemental kingdoms, and our higher selves, who are here to help guide us embody our full potential in each moment within our own human experience, guide us to greater perspectives, and enlighten our daily lives as beings grounded here on Earth.

The cards you draw match your energetic vibration in the present moment and the messages you attract will be for you, based on the Law of Attraction. The process of card pulling requires you to open your inner sense of intuition, enabling you to navigate the process.

CLEAR YOUR CARDS

Your cards are sensitive to vibrations and will have taken in energy from wherever they have been whilst making their way to you. This means that it is important to give your deck an energetic cleanse before you use it. This process ensures the deck is free from any old or stagnant energy, whether from yourself or others during previous readings, or from the environment. By clearing this energy, you can receive guidance that is channelled directly to you. Here are some simple ways to clear your cards:

- Hold the deck in your non-dominant hand, and with your dominant hand, knock on it three times, like you would on a door. Be firm, yet gentle.

- You can also cleanse your deck by lighting (ethically sourced) sage, palo santo, or incense and pass the smoke over the cards.
- One further way of clearing your cards is to ground them with the earth by placing them under a tree or on the grass for a few minutes, to rebalance their energies.

PREPARING YOURSELF

When you are ready, ground yourself to the earth below, clear your mind, and hold your deck of cards at your heart-centre whilst closing your eyes. Take a few deep breaths and ask a question. You might ask for a daily message that you wish to receive, or for some guidance or perspective on whatever is weighing on you. Alternatively, you can ask multiple questions under the energy of a particular card spread. You can ask out loud, or in your mind. Now shuffle your cards and pay attention to the feelings you pick up whilst doing so — any sensations, thoughts, or visions. Stop once you think the time is right; there is no 'right' time, trust you will stop shuffling when you're meant to.

CHOOSING A CARD

You may feel drawn to pick the card at the top, or cut the deck wherever feels right. Or you may wish to spread the cards out in front of you with the pictures and words lying face-down before choosing. Try not to think too much about which card(s) to pick, as your intuition will always draw you to the right message. Allow yourself to follow your intuition and go with the flow of your emotions. Tune in to the energies of each option and move towards the direction that resonates with you the most. You may also feel drawn to more than one card — that's okay; pick as many as are calling to you. There are no mistakes, you can't pick a wrong card. Your inner knowing is stronger than any of your five human senses alone. Have faith that whatever you receive is exactly what you need in this moment.

You may also have times when the cards you pull make little sense to your current phase of life. Don't be confused — the cards will reveal their truth to you in good time when you eventually connect the dots. They might just be coming to you as a heads-up message for what is coming soon, something that your guidance team wants to alert you about.

Card Spreads

Using different spreads empowers you to delve deeper into the essence of your questions, providing you with a comprehensive understanding of the intricacies at play. Readings can be generalised towards any question that is present in the moment. Specialised spreads address particular questions you have or focus on specific areas of life. By employing various spreads, you embark on an exploration that goes beyond the surface and into different dimensions of a situation, gain deeper understanding, and uncover new layers of meaning.

ONE-CARD DRAW (CARD OF THE DAY)

A card-of-the-day oracle reading involves drawing a single card to receive guidance, insight, or inspiration for the day ahead. It is a simple and quick practice that can offer a focal point or theme for you to focus on throughout the day.

THREE-CARD SPREAD (PAST, PRESENT, FUTURE)

1. **Card One: Past** — Acknowledges your past and what lessons you have been working on.

2. **Card Two: Present** — Holds information about the present moment, what you are working on, learning, and what you should know right now.

3. **Card Three: Future** — Shows what you need to know about your very near future (up to three months). It also may show you what you need to do to bring about the situation you desire.

FOUR-CARD SPREAD (DAILY)

Using a daily four-card oracle spread can be a supportive practice to gain more in-depth guidance for your day ahead. Each card represents a specific aspect that can provide valuable information for navigating daily challenges and maintaining alignment.

1. **Card One:** Challenge for the day
2. **Card Two:** Energy to use today
3. **Card Three:** Energy to avoid today
4. **Card Four:** How to stay most in alignment today

THE FIVE-ELEMENTS SPREAD

The Five-Elements Spread is an advanced reading that deeply connects with the energy of this deck.

Create an alchemical element star by assembling, twigs, and flower stems, or opt for a simple drawing on a large piece of paper.

Divide your oracle deck into five distinct stacks, aligning each stack with the corresponding colour of its element: green cards for Earth, royal blue cards for Air, yellow cards for Fire, light blue cards for Water, and purple cards for Spirit.

Shuffle each small stack until you feel an intuitive sense to stop. Turn over the top card and carefully position it according to the corresponding placement on the following page:

1. **Card One: Earth** — Represents your foundation, or sense of stability with finances, work, family, and home.

2. **Card Two: Air** — Shows your current relationship to change, travel, and your imagination.

3. **Card Three: Fire** — Represents your sense of self, your confidence, and your desires and goals.

4. **Card Four: Water** — Corresponds to the currents of your emotional world and the health of relationships.

5. **Card Five: Spirit** — Represents your affinity to the infinite and your spirituality.

The Golden Key of Earth

The *Golden Key of Earth*, concealed in the north, possesses the transformative power to unlock profound qualities of stability and grounding, and teaches us to nurture a deep connection to the physical realm. As we turn this key, we awaken a deep appreciation for the earth's abundant gifts, cultivating patience and a sense of inner balance and security.

Just as the earth sustains and nurtures all living beings, the *Golden Key of Earth* invites us to nourish ourselves and extend that nourishment to others, much like the way trees interconnect and communicate through their mycelial networks. Through the whispers of these ancient arboreal beings, we learn the importance of presence, simplicity, and honouring our roots and heritage. As our consciousness alters, we unearth the profound connection we share with the sacred land, revealing its true depth.

1. Communication
Don't be afraid to express how you really feel.

CARD WISDOM

Trees thrive and forests survive because they synergise together in a loving community — working as one, to look after one another, and to meet all needs. They do this through wondrous communication both under and over the ground, but without words and body language, unlike how we humans communicate; so it seems secret to us.

Above the ground, they use stimuli such as scents, sounds, and signals to fight off any incoming attacks. This interaction warns neighbouring trees of potential threats or pests lurking within their forest. They share seeds which the wind and the birds carry away to birth new life into their ever-growing tree tribe.

Underground, trees communicate through the mycelium fungi roots acting as threads. Just like how thousands of nerves connect the human brain together, roots of a tree work similarly with this interconnected network of nodes. These thread nodes connect one tree-root system to another tree-root system, so that nutrients, carbon, and water can exchange between the trees — like an underground pipeline, some roots even travel hundreds of kilometres. The trees share resources whenever necessary and protect each other from disease. Not only that, but the fungi also help shield the plants from infections through the protective compounds in their roots. This 'wood-wide web' is an integral part of instant communication from near and far.

In human communities, older people share their knowledge and wisdom with the young. Mother trees—also known as hubs—help the younger trees in their surroundings, even sending out messages to the younger ones before they die.

We can learn much from the trees by maintaining healthy communication in our own community. One key lesson we can take away is that trees do not compete with one another for resources, they cooperate. Even if they are shading their neighbours, they still send them resources like carbon, nutrients, and water. They don't compete to be the tallest or the mightiest or keep all their resources or information to themselves; they share what they have to help the whole. There is no competition, only compassion. We too must ourselves to receive offers of help when we need them. Giving and receiving in total harmony brings great health and strength to ourselves and to the collective community of all.

INVITATION

Honest communication is key now in order to improve your current situation. You are being guided to align yourself with the natural rhythms and cycles of your life — cycles which urge you to communicate your own truth with clarity and authenticity. Don't just assume that others know what you want or understand how you truly feel. Embrace speaking your truth without seeking approval from others or holding back out of the fear you won't be accepted. You don't need to blame or accuse anyone, just state your case clearly. Know that it is an act of love to communicate clearly, lovingly, and honestly. You cannot lose anything by simply stating your truth or asking for help. Through this process you will honour and empower yourself, as well as earn much love and respect from those around you. Have faith that stating what is right for you will serve the greater good of all.

If you have something important to say, you are being supported, now, to openly communicate or express your feelings in whatever way feels true to you! This could be through writing, poetry, speaking, art, music, or any medium you wish. Whether your message serves as medicine to inspire those around you or to heal yourself, recognise its essential role in elevating not only your own vibration but also the collective global consciousness. Whatever you voice to others, you may also need to be reminded of your own words. Give—and also receive—your own guidance, wisdom, and hope; how you treat a friend is also how you should treat and speak to yourself. Listen to your own advice!

2. Grounding
Recentre yourself by grounding your energy.

CARD WISDOM

Spirituality guides us to expand our awareness beyond our physical bodies and the material world, enabling us to transcend into elevated states of consciousness. Although floating heavenwards is pleasant and makes us feel more closely connected to the Divine, we are born into these 'soul suits' to undergo a human experience; we have important work to do upon these grounds.

For some people, connecting with the earth doesn't come naturally and requires a conscious effort to learn. This is often the case for people who resonate with the energy of 'star souls', 'star seeds' or 'indigos', and those who simply just don't feel like they belong here on Earth. Nearly all star souls feel more comfortable in an ethereal state of consciousness than a third-dimensional one. They usually discover early in life that they can easily dissociate from being human. This creates an unsteady state of being ungrounded.

Daydreaming keeps us vacant from living in the here and now. Drifting into different dimensions of time and space, we lose ourselves in a trance of otherness, yearning to relive past memories or hasten the future. The worries about what lies ahead or what has passed can tear us away from the present moment. If we keep our energy absent from the moment we are living in, we cannot anchor our highest visions into our bodies.

Standing trees embody the strong balance between the heavens and the earth. They are rooted into the soil, taking in their nourishment from Mother Earth, and freely giving back to us all with their oxygen offerings and their branches reaching out to praise Father Sky. They share the gifts they have been born here to give, with us and the rest of the world.

We are all spiritual beings having a human experience. By maintaining a deep connection with Mother Gaia, we can unlock a plethora of valuable insights. This connection not only allows us to understand ourselves better, but also helps us comprehend the world on a deeper level too. To fully experience the richness of this human existence in our present reality, we must love reality more than fantasy. We must fuse our experience of higher consciousness with a connection to Earth, otherwise we are just floating around like a seed in the wind — filled with infinite potential and not serving its full purpose until it is deeply rooted in the soil. Our spiritual experiences can be amazing too and bring about powerful realisations; but if we let ourselves drift aimlessly, lost in the ether, our efforts to birth our creations will become fruitless — unless we give them firm ground to land upon.

INVITATION

Your mind has been too scattered lately. You are spending too much time living in your mind and higher realms, rather than living fully in your body. Come back to Earth and reground yourself. Mother Gaia is yearning for you to reconnect with her, to connect deeper to yourself and all life around you. Your body is composed of the materials of the earth. Disconnection from your physical self can cause disconnection from the entirety of your being, including your mind and soul. This brings about a great feeling of misalignment. When your mind becomes scattered your actions become ineffective. By keeping a strong connection to the earth, you will feel more stable and balanced within your life. It will give you a quiet solidity from which thoughts gain clarity and actions come from a place of focused intent. You will become more present.

There are many methods to ground yourself. One powerful technique is called 'earthing', which improves your personal bond with Mother Earth. Walk barefoot and imagine etheric roots growing from the soles of your feet and extending into the ground. Follow your breath, so each time you exhale, you imagine these roots extending even deeper. Each time you inhale, draw up the loving, nurturing power of Pachamama, and with every exhale release onto her what is heavy on your heart — breathe it all out and put down what you are carrying. Take time to ground and recentre yourself within the elements and know that Gaia always embraces you.

3. Patience

**Patience is your virtue now. You are almost there!
Keep sowing seeds of love.**

CARD WISDOM

We are all born from the earth, and to her we return. Between and throughout our existence here, we are but the gardeners. Just as we tend to the soil to cultivate crops for sustenance, we must also nurture the gardens of our minds, cultivating a serene sanctum both within ourselves and in our surroundings. By doing so, we can reap a bountiful harvest of love and joy in our everyday lives, in all ways.

We must treat our delicate minds as gardens and our thoughts as seeds. We can either grow a mind full of flowers or a mind tangled in weeds. Which is why we must be mindful of what we want our minds *full* of. Our minds are fertile—yet fragile—grounds, but with the power to give birth to great things!

The primary purpose of a seed is to grow into a new tree, create beautiful flowers, and deliver juicy fruits. When we begin on the spiritual path, we plant new seeds of knowledge and ideas into our mind-garden. When watered well with attention and intention, these seeds grow strong roots over time which coil down the spine and into the earth, into the soil and deep into our soul. We become a special, spiritual tree with deeper, stronger roots that are not crippled by storms. We provide shade to lost souls, so that they too can stand tall and strong and serve their purpose as guardians.

When we travel on a spiritual path, we sometimes meet with frustration. Learning new ways of experiencing the world in a whole new light can crack open the shell of our hearts and fill us with an overwhelming sense of joy and peace. We want to share this enlightening way with the rest of the world and the ones we love most. However, a battle can begin when others aren't there to meet us where we are at; not seeing or understanding in the way we wish them too. We cannot force someone to hear a message they are not ready to receive. Trying to deeply explain concepts of spirituality to those not consciously on the same path is like trying to explain colours to a sightless person. Nonetheless, there is so much magic held in a tiny seed. Small, dormant, still — yet filled with infinite, incredible potential. We should never underestimate the power of a seed once planted.

We are constantly planting seeds in other people's mind-gardens and the world. We, as individuals, hold the power to influence every thought we think, word we speak, action we take, and step we make. Through our conscious choices we leave a lasting imprint in the universe, recognising that our existence holds significant meaning and impact.

INVITATION

You are almost at the finish line!

Have patience with your progress; understand that things are happening, even when you can't see clear results yet. Work began when your recent actions planted a seed. Remember, a seed knows how to wait ... a seed is alive whilst it waits. Trust that work is being done beneath the surface, and soon you will witness the blossoming of your efforts. It is important to continue putting in effort, but avoid pushing or rushing anything, as disrupting the natural flow of events will not yield any benefits. Just as you wouldn't pick unripe fruit from a tree, timing is crucial, and there is so much to gain from your efforts. Remember, patience pays off — good things come to those who wait.

You are also being asked to plant new seeds in your mind for a positive mindset, and pull out any weeds (negative thoughts) that are causing inner turmoil. Perhaps clear your mind using meditation, let go of all the negative vegetation, or set yourself a positive intention for the day.

Ask yourself or journal on these prompts:

- What parts of yourself are you leaving to rot?
- What parts of yourself need to be watered with more love?
- What negative self-talk and self-doubts need to be weeded and cleared from your mind?

Watering your mind with daily doses of affectionate inspiration is an essential form of inner gardening work. To blossom into the person you aspire to be, you must understand your needs and take actions accordingly. Just like tending to any plant, you must provide it with the right environment and care for that species in order for it to thrive, otherwise it will wilt and wither. It is crucial now to cultivate patience and persistence. Identify who you wish to become and take specific actions to align yourself with your unique needs. From here, you will flourish into the best version of yourself!

Share any new spiritual wisdom you've attained with other 'brain backyards' and help spread the sprouting of loving guidance. Be mindful not to be too strong or too forceful — minds are delicate places, and too much force will only cause havoc, especially if you enter as an intruder to private property. Just drop gently, well-intended knowledge seeds over the fence and let the divine light take over. Your job is done.

4. Patterns

Look at the patterns in your life and alter your perspective to see the world in a different light. Be willing to change or modify your behaviour.

CARD WISDOM

The word 'art' is at the heart of the word 'e**art**h'. Mother nature's creation is nothing short of a sublime masterpiece! She painted our world with such vibrancy and saturated all of it in patterns that play off of each other — some linear, some circular, and some arbitrary, or a combination of all three. Occasionally they are obvious and sometimes they require creative exploration to locate, with only a little effort. From the extraordinary tessellations within hexagonal honeycomb, to the fascinating geometry of seashells, snowflakes, or a hallucinatory head of a Romanesco broccoli, the wonders of nature offer different perspectives on the world.

However, amid our fast-paced materialistic lifestyles, we overlook these delicate complexities.

The magnificence of the world can easily lose its allure because of its surface level familiarity. When we view the natural world through a superficial lens, it lacks depth. This shallow perspective mirrors itself within our own psyche, reflecting the shallowness of our own relationships and willingness to understand others. We only meet others as deeply as we meet ourselves; similarly, we only meet life as deeply as we have met ourselves. The illumination of our own self-awareness reveals the sanctity that surrounds us, enabling us to rediscover and re-remember the holiness within ourselves and all things. This transformation of perception allows us to experience the world forever anew, with a sense of wonder and awe, like a newborn infant discovering the world for the first time.

Despite the vast array of human creations surrounding us—be it a woven basket, a car, a building, a delicate croissant, or a milliner's bowler hat— it is just *earth* reworked, an image brought forth from the 'image-nation' of someone's imagination, to create more art from their heart to add to the earth.

From thought to form, we encode love into what we create, adding to the ever-expansiveness of our universe. We must meet with, and witness, this labour of love in all that's around us in this physical realm.

Whenever you encounter a creation, approach it with a sense of presence and awareness, embracing the beauty and craftsmanship within it. From the clothes you wear to the packaging of your coffee, from the design of your duvet to the music that fills your ears, each carries a story of dedication and passion. Can you feel the pure joy and excitement that emanates from a musician when they release the new track you're listening to? Or the exhilaration felt by an author when their book you're now reading receives recognition for publication, after years of dedicated writing? And let's not forget all the souls toiling behind the scenes—like the meticulous music producers and insightful book editors in these cases, alongside everybody else—whose contributions are indispensable in bringing these artistic creations to life. Let us appreciate the hours, the sweat, and the love poured into these efforts, celebrating the fruits of their labour and the impact they have on our lives.

Have you ever taken a moment to recognise the depth of what goes into the meal you order at a restaurant? Instead of mindlessly consuming your food, pause to savour the delicious flavours and appreciate the human effort behind it. Consider the journey that led these ingredients to your plate and acknowledge the hard work of the farmers who nurtured them. Reflect on the love, dedication, and patience invested, from a tiny seed's journey to its full bloom. This single dish represents a culmination of many lifeforms' lifelong labours, offering you but a moment of delightful satisfaction.

Nature gives its whole life with pleasure for our joy and satisfaction in mostly all that we own. We cannot miss this motive. Perception blended together with much gratitude creates a vast portal that changes our whole lives—as quick as a flick of a switch from darkness to light—allowing us to see things more clearly.

INVITATION

Take a step back and look at the bigger picture of your life. Notice the patterns, particularly how you relate to everything in your world and what drives you to attract the sorts of people and experiences you do. Reflect on recurring themes, dynamics, and triggers in your interactions.

Write down specific examples that come to mind. This self-reflection provides valuable insights.

Pay attention to what these patterns might show you. They could highlight areas for personal growth and development. For instance, consistently attracting partners who lack trust may indicate a need to cultivate self-trust. If you find yourself repeatedly drawn to relationships with compromised boundaries, it's an invitation to prioritise and assert your own needs. By recognising and embracing the lessons embedded in these patterns, you can break free from repetitive cycles and move towards healthier relationships.

Once you have gained clarity on these patterns and lessons, it's time to modify your behaviour for better outcomes. This requires self-awareness, willingness to change, and a commitment to personal growth. Consider practical steps you can take to change your behaviour, such as setting boundaries, practising effective communication, nurturing self-love and self-care, or seeking support from a trusted friend, therapist, or coach.

In challenging situations, rise above and gain perspective. Imagine observing yourself from a higher vantage point, seeing your life and interactions with others. This shift in perspective helps problems appear smaller and allows you to recognise behavioural patterns more clearly. You can even zoom out further and imagine viewing yourself from the perspective of the universe to gain a sense of the bigger picture and the insignificance of your worries in the grand scheme of things. This understanding opens your heart, which supports you to connect with others and make a real difference in their lives. It also brings inner peace as you realise the preciousness of your time on Earth, prompting you to let go and love more.

Change your gaze and release the 'me against them' mindset. Try to empathise and see things from others' point of view. Let go of intense and overwhelming emotions, replacing them with understanding and love. This transmutation of feelings brings about a purer, lighter dimension of expression. When you change your perception and break destructive behaviour patterns, you rewire the chemistry of your body and rewrite your life.

5. Growth

Invest in yourself and make necessary changes within your external environment to help you grow.

CARD WISDOM

For a seed to become its greatest expression and to reach its ultimate potential, it must first be buried in total darkness and broken apart. The shell shakes and its insides burst out. To someone who doesn't grasp the manner of growth, it looks like total havoc! Much the same with inner work — sometimes it takes being immersed in the dark spaces of life, with our hearts broken and our worlds completely shaken, for us to crack open and grow into a more beautiful, blossoming version of self.

As the gardeners of our own minds, we delve inward to tend to our inner mind-garden. The more we go inward and nurture our garden, uprooting the destructive weeds from the foundation—the toxic inner dialogue, self-limiting beliefs, and trash self-talk—the more we make space to plant new seeds of love. By gently tending to our inner garden daily, we witness the beautiful blossoming of our greatest expressions of self.

As any dedicated gardener knows, creating a sanctum takes patience, dedication, and hard work. We endure the mud, blood, sweat, and tears we push through, even when things look messier and more chaotic than they did at the beginning. We invest in the tools to get the job done efficiently. Most importantly, the work is consistent over time, otherwise nothing will change or grow.

Once our seeds start to finally bloom and we bear the fruits of our efforts, we are then able to revel in all the beauty, enjoying and sharing the succulent rewards. There is joy in witnessing it all blossom outwardly from our hearts and into existence. Then all we need is manageable maintenance work to ensure the garden is kept tidy, weed-free, and a pleasurable place to be. Whenever something needs our attention and tending to, we have the right tools and skills available in our mind-shed, ready to apply — e.g., mindfulness, meditation, mindset hacks, gratitude, journalling, affirmations, visualisations, breathwork, therapy tools, etc.

As this historic proverb suggests, "The kingdom of heaven is within you, and whoever shall know oneself, shall find it."

INVITATION

When you find yourself in a situation where you are not thriving emotionally, energetically, or financially, look at the soil you are planted in. What do you need to adjust in your external reality to live in optimal conditions?

Imagine that you have a plant that is not thriving, do you blame the plant, or do you instead look at the environment and find out what is missing? You do what is necessary to better its conditions and help it flourish — is it getting too little or too much? How are the nutrients in the soil, is it well fed? Is there too little or too much light? Are there weeds, pests, or toxins around, threatening its health?

This card reminds you that you are not the problem, neither are you to blame, but you must take responsibility to change things. Are you getting enough fresh water, enough sunlight? How are your living situations? Do you feel rooted in your job or are you rotting? What is toxic in your life — a habit, or a person? Look at what you are consuming — are you living in healthy conditions or are destructive cycles leaving you dormant? Look at what is around you and change your reality by changing your surroundings. You cannot grow by staying stuck in dark places — just like seeds under the soil need to be tended to with love and a plant needs to be cared for.

The essence of the earth element acknowledges that you put others before yourself; but it is time to put yourself first for a change. Call upon the energy of the earth and your spirit guides to hold and support you at any moment. Nourish your roots to show up as the strongest and very best you can be. By investing in yourself and utilising appropriate tools— such as working with a coach, seeking counselling, reading specific books, attending relevant classes, receiving massages, or practising self-care techniques—you can experience significant personal growth. These actions can provide the nourishment and support needed to thrive in various aspects of your life. The results may include enhanced self-awareness, improved skills, increased wellbeing, and a greater sense of fulfilment.

Gratitude
Be grateful for what you have.

6. Gratitude
Be grateful for what you have.

CARD WISDOM

It is impossible to meet with Native American traditional wisdom and ceremonies and ignore the immensity of the gratitude expressed. This gratitude is a gentle, quiet form that runs root deep into the earth's soil. It sits in the still lakes. It touches peaked mountain tops, circling high with the hawks in the skies. It even reaches further above, to celestial spaces within the beyond, and further below into the underworld. The spiritual and ecological dimensions of relations between human and non-human beings within native cultural heritage, always begin with gratitude. These communities begin their expressions of gratitude by acknowledging and giving thanks for all aspects of nature, ranging from the celestial stars above to the very earth beneath their feet. They hold the earth in deep reverence, seeing it all as sacred. Equally they treat it that way, honouring all that is, and honouring the nature spirits that dwell in the in-between too. They give thanks to their people, their families, their ancestors, and—above all—to the Creator of All.

The bison is a symbol of gratitude for the Lakota People. Hunting them is a mindful act, utilising every part of the animal—meat, hide, and bones—with deep appreciation for its abundant gifts. The bison is seen as a sacred 'brother', vital for survival. Before hunting, the Lakota seek permission from the bison spirit and offer gratitude for its provision, reciprocating with their own offerings, such as sacred herbs or tobacco. The same respect is shown when harvesting plants. The Lakota People believe that the right action accompanied by the right prayer ensures survival without struggle. The prayers of Indigenous people around the world embody reverence for the earth and the thoughtful honouring of animal lives by taking only what is necessary.

For many of us, Gaia's gifts have become commodities, packaged in foam trays and wrapped in plastic, paired with a price tag for us to buy and eat. We must pay for her water, her trees are cut down and sold for dining tables, her flowers are pulled out and profited from, and her land bought and sold. Here lies the disconnect — objects bought and sold aren't necessarily regarded the same as gifts which are precious, given with much to cherish.

Over time, we have lost the deep connection we once had with our Great Mother. Market-driven economies not only perpetuate inequality and disparity for the sake of human convenience but also wreak havoc on the natural world. We have severed the reciprocal relationship of giving and receiving with her. We take abundantly—often beyond what we truly need—without offering our sincere gratitude in return. Contrast this with our ancestors, whose lives were intimately intertwined with the land; their understanding of the world as a gift was inherent, effortless and obvious.

A gift relationship with nature is an intimate one which acknowledges our participation and our dependence upon it. One where we see ourselves as part of nature, not alien to it. Gift exchange with Gaia is the commerce of choice. It harmonises with the process of natural abundance and will only forever flourish with reciprocated love and gratitude. Let us pray that we all remember and return to our roots of deep reverence for the earth, just as our ancestors did.

INVITATION

Shower your life with gratitude in all areas that seem dry and unloved. Watch the fruits of your efforts blossom into full flower as abundance extends more of this bountiful love back into your life. Share recognition of all those loved ones in your life—upon the earth or in spirit—who have helped form who you are now. Write a list of all the things you are grateful for in your life in this present moment. Reflection and contemplation awaken thoughts of remembrance that acknowledge your connection to All That Is.

Before each meal, take a moment to pause before you eat, and express gratitude for the food on your plate. Acknowledge the effort and resources that went into growing, harvesting, delivering, and preparing the meal. Consider supporting local and sustainable food sources whenever possible.

Extend your grace towards Gaia by organising or joining a community clean-up event or simply picking up trash whenever you visit natural spaces. Take a leisurely walk in a nearby park, immersing yourself in nature's beauty. Express gratitude for the trees, plants, animals, and the environment. When you feel inclined to pick a flower or harvest from the wild, offer a strand of your hair as a reciprocal gesture. This act mirrors the connection between plucking a stem and tugging a strand of hair —a shared sensation from each respective roots, that reminds us of our symbiotic relationship with the earth. By giving a part of yourself, you actively contribute to the cycle of life. As the hair decomposes, it enriches the soil with nutrients, nourishing the plants. You become an integral part of the intricate web of life, offering a profound and tangible gift to the earth.

Choosing this card brings a message of appreciation from the higher realms to your heart. Give thanks for your miraculous beating heart and the energy it moves through your body. Open your heart, developing the intelligence within to deepen your connection to life with oneness and awe. Show gratitude to your body for all it does. Thank your feet for supporting you and your hands for channelling the magic of spirit. Thank your cells for fighting diseases, rooting for you each day. It's easy to fall into self-judgment and self-pity, forgetting the miracle of being alive, breathing, feeling, and experiencing in this earthly life.

Appreciating the divine nature of you and everything around you expands your awareness and gratitude for All That Is. Embrace this practice of gratitude, recognising the vital role you play in the ecosystem and the unity that binds all beings together.

7. Wisdom

You are being guided to learn something new to expand your mind and consciousness — whether a skillset-based study or the act of self-study.

CARD WISDOM

Not all schools have four walls and not all textbooks are paged books. We live upon a wide-open workbook that is laid upon our lands, that is written in the waves of our seas for us to sink our eyes and hearts deeply into, authored by our Earth Mother. Instead of reading symbols, we must learn to read the subtle, the unspoken, and unseen — reading between the lines of form and the formless within the living world.

Through the five elements, Gaia demonstrates through example. Her syllabus of the seasons teaches us how to navigate our inner processes and truly be who we are — that is, to be in an open and ever-changing exercise of self-expression. She teaches us about limits, as well as possibilities: patience, hard work, peace, renewal, abundance, generosity, kindness, acceptance, self-reliance, and much more if we are willing to pay attention and learn. Her lessons are not taught under a roof. Traditional learning, thus far, has only served useful to humanity by helping us attain 'good' jobs and fitting us into a closed-minded society, in order to maintain outer self-growth stemming from egoic desires. Nature's school is under the stars, graded not by numbers but the awakening of one's heart and mind through the study, progress, and process of our own soul and inner self-growth.

Earth's wisdom surpasses human comprehension, emanating from entities even wiser than the highest mountains and oldest trees. Wisdom resides not only within individuals but also finds embodiment in the ancient oak tree, a venerable guardian of ancestral knowledge in the Western tradition. Like the steadfast human keepers of wisdom, these majestic beings house within their bark and branches vast libraries of knowledge, history, and Earth's mysteries. They stand as a testament to the profound wisdom held by non-human entities, illustrating that Gaia's wisdom stems from ancestral and universal sources.

The Hopi People, native to the southwestern United States, regard owls as carriers of wisdom and knowledge. These silent birds of prey are believed to possess deep insight and intuition, offering guidance and understanding to those who seek it. They are believed to be of a watchful and vigilant nature, embodying the wisdom of the ancestors, acting as spiritual protectors and carriers of messages between different realms of existence. Hopi elders graciously act as the messengers for these messenger owls. Through the art of storytelling and the power of their teachings, these wise elders ensure that the profound medicine of the owls continues to resonate and uplift individuals within the Hopi community and beyond.

For the wise person, knowledge is not acquired — it is transmitted. They are repositories of memories, keepers of learning, and vessels for higher knowledge to enter. Learning is passed down and instructed mostly through example, guided by the wisdom of elders or by the lessons taught by nature. Earth serves as our direct home-school, Gaia masters her own teachings from the higher university of the universe. We are perpetual students of life, continuously learning through introspection and exploration of the world around us. The knowledge we seek should be driven by intentions that surpass personal wealth and material gain. Instead, our desires should focus on expanding consciousness and deepening self-awareness. We exist as both students and teachers, capable of supporting ourselves and guiding others on their journey back to the heart. As Ram Dass wisely said, "We're all just walking each other home." This is the essence of our shared path.

INVITATION

Embrace this pivotal moment in your soul's journey, as new opportunities for growth and learning arise. Expand your consciousness by acquiring fresh ideas and skills. Consider enrolling in classes, exploring books, or seeking online workshops. This pursuit may guide you towards a fulfilling career aligned with your purpose, bringing enrichment to your life and the lives of others. Share your knowledge with others, as teaching and learning form a symbiotic cycle. By imparting wisdom on topics that ignite your passion, you awaken joy within yourself and reinforce your own lessons.

In challenging times, remember that life's lessons involve both successes and setbacks. Be kind to yourself and shift your perspective on difficulties. Rather than viewing them as failures, see them as chances for profound soul growth. Let mistakes inspire personal growth, guiding you to shed unwanted aspects and align with your true self.

8. Compassion

Show compassion now, dear one, and try to understand another's point of view.

CARD WISDOM

Compassion is the crown of all virtues. It is the quality that takes us closest to the Divine within each of us. When we live with compassion at the forefront of everything we do, our life is led with love. Compassion is the outgrowth of love; love is the outgrowth of understanding; and understanding is the outgrowth of purpose. Compassion is considered to be a very advanced spiritual quality. It gives the power to psychically penetrate into the core of existence, instilling within us a reverence for all life, all living organisms, whether animate or inanimate.

Being compassionate is about accepting others exactly as they are, meeting them where they are at in their lives, and *seeing* them completely. In the Zulu tradition, the word *sawubona* meaning 'I see you; I accept you just as you are' offers an intention to release any preconceptions and judgements. It represents the Zulu philosophy of *ubuntu*, translating as 'humanity towards all' — a spiritual ethic advocating mutual support for bringing each other into existence. *Ubuntu* is the recognition that we are all bound in ways that can be invisible to the eye, that there is a oneness to humanity, and that we achieve more by sharing ourselves with others and caring for those around us.

Compassion helps us to be gentle with ourselves, to forgive our humanness and our past selves when we make mistakes, and to forgive others too. Everyone is on their own outer and inward spiritual journey, whether or not they are aware of it. Everyone experiences life differently and sees it through a totally different lens of perception to our own. Compassion helps us to understand another's view and to really *see* them, beyond their human form. Not from you and me, but rather, I and we — the unity of souls and realignment with the mass consciousness in which we all are one and the same.

The spiritual practice of compassion entails opening the heart and allowing us to feel the suffering in the world, including our own, without turning away from pain, but moving towards it with open arms. It involves seeing everything and everyone through the eyes of love — including ourselves and all creatures, both in nature and the inanimate world.

INVITATION

This card is a message to treat others as you would like to be treated. Be mindful as you go about your day and in your interactions with others. Remember, the Universal Law of Cause and Effect states that what you put out is what you get back. If you feel you are not being treated fairly by others, take a moment to tune in to your heart centre and notice how you might demonstrate 'compassion in action' at that moment. How you act (and react) affects everyone and everything in your life. It serves as a guiding principle shaping the course of your experiences, leading to either more positive or negative outcomes. Just as a wheel turns, symbolising the continuous flow of life's events, your karmic cycles represent the interconnected nature of your actions and their consequences.

You are encouraged to open your heart and mind and see others through the eyes of love, in order to improve your current situation. Engage in a perspective-taking exercise by imagining yourself in someone else's situation — put yourself in their shoes and consider their everyday experiences, challenges, and emotions. Through this practice, you will cultivate empathy, foster understanding, and refine your communication skills. Discover the power of conflict resolution and relationship building, as you forge deeper connections and nurture personal growth. By embracing empathy, you unlock the potential for greater harmony and connection across all aspects of your life. Be receptive and attuned to others, seeking to understand their unique perspectives. As you expand your understanding, your consciousness expands. New pathways emerge, paving the way for the manifestation of your dreams and the healing of the situation. Approach with keen observation and non-judgement, for therein lies the key to your success.

Just as you are being asked to show compassion for others, do not forget to be compassionate and gentle with yourself; for this is also true: how we treat ourselves is how we will allow others to treat us.

9. Give Yourself a Break

You are a human being not a human doing.
Don't be so hard on yourself; give yourself a break.

CARD WISDOM

Life is not a problem to be solved or a competition to be won, it's a sensation to be felt — like walking barefoot on soft soil and the warmth of sunlight kissing your face. So many rush around in a great panic, feeling under pressure to achieve all sorts to give them a sense of reason, beyond just having life and having breath. This is more than enough to give us meaning to exist; it is plenty.

The words 'human being' clarify that our primary focus should be on the *being* and not the *doing*. If we were 'human doings', it would be acceptable for us to live like machines and be constantly working to serve some system. But we are born to serve a higher purpose — to tend to the inner self.

Unfortunately, our busy society today has us moving faster, as if we were born to be robots, and does not look to be slowing down anytime soon. Emails fill up our inboxes daily, and we all have a constant to-do list. Outer pressures keep us perpetually entangled in the pursuit of external validation, material possessions, and societal expectations. We are led to believe that the key to success and wealth lies solely in constant *doing*, rather than in the success of our inner growth and happiness. With this comes the attitude that we must 'earn' our rest only after exhausting ourselves first, and if we are not constantly working and being productive, we are seen to be lazy and meaningless. We do not see any other life form live by this order of hurry. While we may need to live this way to a degree, we should not be in such a hurry that we forget our essence as humans in this experience.

In nature, we see nothing ever worrying or hurrying, yet everything is always on time and accomplished. The fauna and flora flourish in their own essence of being, without doubts, fear, or misery of not being enough. They move in the present and feel into each passing moment. Instead of measuring our days by the amount of work we complete, we should focus on the quality of our presence in each moment and strive to experience life to the fullest. We must stop allowing productivity to be the dictator of our worth.

When we focus on *being*, we experience lasting love, peace, and happiness. Our thoughts, words, and actions likewise reflect this focus, and our state becomes unaffected by people and situations. However, if we stay hyperfixated on accomplishments, validation, relationships, and situations, our peace and happiness will not last, as these aspects of life are not in our control.

While it is important to acknowledge and value our accomplishments, possessions, and relationships as parts of our purpose and sacred duty, it is crucial to prioritise our highest purpose, which is to nurture and care for our inner selves.

INVITATION

Drawing this card suggests you have been putting too much pressure on yourself. You have been doing too much whilst taking in lots of new information. You need to hit the pause button to absorb it all and integrate what you have recently learnt. Maybe you feel you have so many tasks to do, the list just keeps on growing, and you don't know where to start or where to stop, and if you stop to rest you will never get through it all. This is causing you mental stress, diminishing your productivity.

Make a space in your mind by creating a priority list and setting yourself realistic expectations. Don't expect too much of yourself. This only leads to overwhelm — you are not a robot, you are trying your best with what you have and know right now, so give yourself a break. You are doing great!

Whether you are on full steam ahead, or stuck in a void of procrastination, you need to take a step back from *doing* for a moment and embrace simply *being*.

Whatever you think you have to finish or accomplish today, it can wait. Make space for some sacred-self time instead and partake in some 'proactive stillness'. To do this, find a quiet and safe space, preferably out in nature, where you can comfortably sit or lie down without distractions. Leave your phone at home or turn it on 'do not disturb' mode. Close your eyes and take some nice deep breaths to relax and ground. Pay attention and feel each breath without controlling it. Notice any thoughts, emotions, or sensations as they arise without judgement, and return your attention to your breath. Expand your awareness to include your bodily sensations or sounds in the environment, and simply observe them without reacting or trying to change them. Stay curious and open to the present moment, accepting whatever arises. If your mind wanders, gently bring it back to the present using your breath as a guide. Practise this for a few minutes or as long as you like.

If all you do today is breathe ... that is enough, and you are achieving great miracles!

Remember, you are a *human being* not a *human doing*.

10. Abundance

You are at a time of harvest!
Get ready to reap the rewards of your efforts.

CARD WISDOM

Abundance is a natural and universal law, and the universe is constantly creating new things. New stars are constantly created, new trees grow, new people are born, and new sources of energy are always being discovered. We are part of this plenitude and can equally create within it.

Abundance and cooperative evolution are interconnected concepts that highlight the potential for growth, progress, and harmony through collaboration and shared resources. Abundance refers to a state of plentifulness, prosperity, and fulfilment in various aspects of life, including material wealth, emotional wellbeing, and spiritual richness. Cooperative evolution emphasises the idea of evolving and advancing together through mutual support and collective efforts.

Abundance doesn't manifest itself from selfish desire. The primary element in everlasting abundance is that of cooperation; the dynamics of which run on the principles of generosity rather than scarcity. In nature, everything works cooperatively; systems of mature coral reefs, old-growth forests, and wild prairies are full of different forms of life. All systems are built on interdependent relationships: flowers provide the pollen and bees are the delivery drivers to dispatch new life; the wind helps spread seeds; trees share nutrients to ensure all in their hub are well fed; ostriches and zebras team up in packs for added protection from predators; and ravens guide wolves to prey. Animals and plants provide their own resources and exist in partnership to maintain a thriving, whole organism — our Earth Mother. While some claim that life boils down to survival of the fittest, in fact, nature advances because of its joint efforts. Just like any successful business or corporation, cooperation lays the groundwork for success. Any good business works as a service provider, which reaps abundant rewards for the whole.

By embracing a mindset of abundance and actively participating in collaborative endeavours, individuals and communities can create thriving environments where talents are utilised, progress is achieved, and everyone's needs are met. This highlights the power of collaboration and sharing resources, ideas, and skills that foster generative change, uplift others, and co-create a better future for all.

INVITATION

Life goes in cycles. There are times when fields lay idle and there are also times of harvest. Right now, you are moving towards a harvest time, so get ready to reap an outpouring of some gain — whether it be money, time, energy, or love.

Be cautious of any unconscious habits that will block your flow to receive. This usually involves self-doubts or complaining about money. Lack mentality will only keep you in a vibration to magnetise more lack. An 'abundance mindset' means that you choose words affirming what you want to call in. Abundance first occurs as thoughts, feelings, and words before this energy materialises. The more you stay in a heightened vibration of love, gratitude, and wholeness, the faster you shall attract your desires.

Nominate yourself as a candidate for increased wealth and prosperity (just like the abundance in nature), and fortune will find a smile on your face too. This doesn't mean that you need to spend lots of money on fashion or fancy things, however it requires you to present as someone who is ambitious and ready to take possession and complete control of their destiny. Become a beaming beauty of gratitude and acknowledge the good that is already in your life. The everlasting stream of abundance is already within you; it is not out *there* somewhere. Keeping a gratitude journal is a wonderful way of reminding yourself how lucky you really are. It will raise your vibration to attract the abundance and prosperity you so desire.

Remember to share the privilege of your abundance with others and know that karma within serves you wonders when you need it most.

The Golden Key of Air

The *Golden Key of Air*, hidden within the East, holds the transformative power to unlock our innate qualities of flexibility, adaptability, and expansive thinking within our consciousness. It symbolises movement, evolution, and inspiration, gently urging us to embrace the winds of change and welcome fresh ideas and diverse perspectives.

Like a gentle breeze that stirs the leaves, the *Golden Key of Air* reminds us of the importance of mental agility and adaptability. It serves as a guiding force, nurturing a flexible mindset and empowering us to take adaptable actions. Even in the fiercest of storms, air softly reminds us to maintain an open-minded approach, a fervent thirst for learning, and the ability to navigate diverse situations with ease.

We find profound beauty in immersing ourselves in the ever-evolving, swirling nature of life — accompanied by the graceful dance and motivating, melodious song of the whispering winds, forever cheering us on.

11. Winds of Change

Great winds of change are forecast ahead, guiding you in a completely new direction. Don't be afraid. Allow yourself to be led by the breeze with ease.

CARD WISDOM

The derivation of the word 'wind' is the same fundamental concept as the words for breath and Great Spirit. The wind blows and moves through space, Great Spirit stirs and enlivens our lifeforce, breath is the bearer of life, bringing oxygen into our bodies. Wind, breath, Great Spirit — all intertwined in one single cosmological framework, all linked, manifesting as the changes the universe embodies.

Humans crave continuity. We cling tenaciously to the illusion that we will get our lives in order and that it will stay that way — but the universe doesn't work that way, and change is the only constant in the cosmos, which is why we must not resist it. If nothing changed, we could not expand consciousness in our lifetime, or learn more about and experience genuine love.

In nature, everything is constantly in motion, cycling through the phases of the seasons — evolving, shedding, renewing. Nothing ever stays the same, and nature lets it all take place without resistance. The trees don't hold on to their leaves for fear of letting go. A bird does not hold on to its young when it's time for them to leave the nest, afraid of them growing up. Recognising the beauty within this impermanence, we open our awareness to the preciousness of everything and every moment.

Change is simply a contrast from our comfortability — and feeling uncomfortable doesn't sit well in our nervous system. As a species, we are creatures of comfort which is why we find it so easy to resist it. Instead of it being something we should fear, we must lean into the discomfort, let go of clinging to the current, and let ourselves be led by the gust of Great Spirit. By going with the wind, we let the love and hand of Great Spirit lead the way.

It would be wise to consider leaving comfort and certainty behind and embrace the winds of change. When we do, the universe leads us to outcomes far greater than what we can immediately understand. Freedom and space to expand open before us.

INVITATION

Give yourself permission to become somebody new.

You may not know it, but every cell in your body is in a perpetual state of regeneration. On a cellular level, your body renews itself on average every 7–10 years. Growth and change are inevitable. Staying the same is impossible.

It is okay to change your mind, it is okay to change direction. Pardon any old parts of yourself that no longer align with who you want to be and allow yourself to begin again. Respect your own natural cycles. Be mindful of seasonal changes and go gracefully with the direction of the wind's whispers and guidance.

Let go of your rigidity of how you want life to unfold, and instead, let yourself be led. If you feel you are chasing something that isn't coming easy, stop chasing, let it go — it is drifting away for a reason. If it is meant to be, it will blow back into your direction when the time is right.

The element of air is guiding you on your path. You are always being held and guided somewhere—and towards something—far greater than you can comprehend. If something is not going your way, lean into your discomfort and detach from holding on to the outcome. Remember, Great Spirit is always holding your hand, like a loving parent or guardian with their child. Trust in their protection.

Gaia, and your guides, want to assure you that everything works out in your favour, even if you cannot quite see it right now.

12. Rainbow Bridge

Embrace your uniqueness to bridge gaps in your life, foster connections, and bring unity and harmony to those around you.

CARD WISDOM

As souls existing in human bodies, we are living in a prism, not a prison. The universal light channels through the inner prism of our consciousness, refracting into a magnificent spectrum of tones, illuminating the world around us, and unveiling our unique radiance. Like sunlight passing through a prism, we are imbued with the vibrant essence of the rainbow — an array of luminosity that defines our being. While we may liken the pure essence of Source energy to white light, it is important to recognise that light transcends mere whiteness — it encompasses the entire spectrum of colours. Similarly, on our spiritual path, while it is crucial to embody the vibrations of light, love, and purity, we must not overshadow the inner interplay of colours within our multifaceted nature. We must let all our colours—our qualities and virtues—shine out through the delicate stained-glass windows of our eyes, revealing our mosaic of colourful emotions and stories. Some may radiate the fiery red of passion, igniting the spirits of those around them with infectious enthusiasm. Others may emanate the tranquil blue of wisdom, offering calm and insight amid uncertainty. The bow of colours we emit is as diverse as the human experience itself, with each individual unveiling their unique, personified palette.

Tiny crystal prisms form rainbows when sunlight meets with water. It is a simple, yet fascinating, blending of elements in perfect visual harmony, creating a road of light magnificently bowing above us in the sky — one of the most beautiful sights in all the world! It is difficult not to be mesmerised at the sight of her majesty when she's beaming right over our heads, like a giant billboard, put in place to grab our attention.

Much like rainbows and the graceful arch of our own smiles, we individually look up to one another with admiration and bridge the gaps that exist in our lives. Through the vibrant colours of our being, we create bridges of connection, understanding, and love. Each hue represents a unique aspect of who we are. These bridges serve as pathways to reach across differences, to mend broken connections, and to bring people closer together. They are bridges of empathy, compassion, and acceptance that span the distances between hearts.

INVITATION

Just as rainbows grace the sky, offering a spectacle of vibrant hues, this card reminds you that you also possess the ability to bridge gaps in your life. Each colour of your being represents a unique aspect of who you are. Through your authentic expression, you create bridges of connection, understanding, and love, spanning the distances between hearts. Like the awe-inspiring rainbow, you are a living prism, refracting the universal light through your consciousness, unveiling your unique radiance to the world. Embrace the diverse mosaic of colours within you, allowing all your qualities and virtues to shine through the delicate stained-glass windows of your soul. As you radiate your true essence, you inspire admiration and bridge the gaps that exist in your life, fostering unity and harmony with those around you.

When something obstructs your progress and prevents you from moving forwards, it's time to cross a bridge or bridge a gap in your life. This transformative act will enable you to leave behind the blockage that has impeded your way. By embarking on this metaphorical crossing, you pave the way for growth and self-discovery, reaching the radiant gold that awaits you as a result of your recent efforts of personal development.

To ensure a successful transition, be clear and resolute in your intentions. Articulate what you desire and communicate your direction to those around you with clarity. Establish firm boundaries, safeguarding yourself against any potential stumbling blocks. This requires reflecting if it is necessary to distance yourself from certain individuals and situations, and effectively severing ties; or tying the relationship ribbon if things need to be mended, fostering reconciliation with people, circumstances, and places. Both choices hold significance in how your continuing journey progresses.

When you come up against any stormy situations, be sure to shine brightly, from the inside out. You will create a rainbow of peace from the bow of your smile and heal the situation by staying in your light. Watch how the atmosphere can change in the room with you shining positivity and being the sun in the situation. The storm meeting your sunlight will weave a beautiful rainbow of peace and hope.

13. Abracadabra

Beware of old wounds resurfacing, and be wise with your words and the spells you cast.

CARD WISDOM

Our words are magic spells ... this is why we 'spell' them and call it 'spelling'. For example, the word 'abracadabra' has several origins, one of which is an Aramaic phrase '*avra kehdabra*' which translates into English as, "I will create as I speak".

In mystical traditions, runes and sigils are powerful tools for spell work. They are symbols embodying ancient wisdom, representing forces of nature, universal energies, and archetypal principles. By understanding and working with runes, we tap into their inherent transformative power, using them for divination, insight, and manifestation. Similar to words, runes carry their own energetic essence and vibrations.

Spells, magic, and curses are often dismissed as fanciful or child's play, but they have historically referred to the art of influencing events using hidden natural forces. Energy—one of the most potent forces on our planet—permeates everything in the universe at different frequencies. Sound directs energy patterns, attracting and flowing like a magnet. Spoken words possess powerful frequencies and vibrations, capable of creating magic beyond what the eye can see. When we speak, we cast our thoughts and vibrations into the earth's magnetic or magic field. Words are our wands, and everything we think or say shapes our reality.

Therefore, we must refrain from speaking negatively about ourselves or others, even as a joke. Our bodies do not know the difference. As children, we learn about the impact of profanity, understanding that cursing is wrong. Yet, people can also cast spells with their words, cursing our reality and making us feel unworthy. A single hurtful comment can crush dreams and alter someone's path forever. We must be mindful of the power our words hold, as they can either inspire or devastate those around us.

INVITATION

Are you consciously creating magic miracles for yourself with your words? Or are you unconsciously cursing your own existence?

This card reveals the message to break any old spells that may be resurfacing. Do not let yourself be hypnotised by the forgery of a worn-out spell — those which have you hypnotised to think that you aren't good enough and those who have controlled you in the past. You are so much more powerful than you think and can defeat them with your wand of willpower. If you want proof, simply look back at all the challenges you have already overcome, just from your action of not giving up. You will also defeat them with the wand of your words.

Make sure the words you speak about yourself are supporting a positive, empowered, and self-confident mindset. These will be your magic spells.

When we carry our wounded ego, we become a walking wound. It's important to remember that others are not actively seeking to hurt us; they are too preoccupied with protecting their own wounds. However, they can project their pain onto us in hurtful ways, enveloping us in a dark magic cloak. It's tempting to cling to our pain as a shield against further misery, but this cloak is deceptive. Holding on to it only generates more suffering within ourselves, trapping us behind a false sense of self. Letting go is the key to freeing ourselves from this cycle.

Place words of affirmation around your home and recite them when you see them, and feel the shift within your own energy from the magic you create. Surround yourself with a protective bubble of healing and love, an energetic shield deflecting or absorbing darkness. Or use sigil magic to enhance your manifestations and bring your desires to life. First, identify your deep desires and intentions. Then, create a unique symbol that represents your intention — this is your sigil. Charge it with your focused energy and purpose, then release it into the universe through burning, burying, or keeping it as a sacred talisman. Trust in the power of your intention and the energy infused in the sigil.

Be mindful of the spells you cast through your words and actions, uplifting and empowering yourself and others. Embrace your role as a magician, using your magic with love and the responsibility to shape your world. Remember, you are constantly shaping your reality with intention and energy.

14. Creative Expression

Connect to your inner child and allow yourself to play and create.

CARD WISDOM

Creative energy, like sexual energy, allows us to 'reproduce' ourselves through creative expression. There is no separation between creator and creation, the dance and the dancer. Together, artists, architects, scientists, engineers, bankers, barbers, gardeners, poets, and parents collaborate to create harmonious and thriving communities through their separate means of purpose. This creative essence extends beyond humanity, embracing all living beings. There is no doubt that there is an undeniable connection between humanity and the natural world. Human voices, with their diverse melodies and expressive tones, serve as an inspiration for the captivating songs of parrots, much like how these enchanting birds inspire artists' paint palettes with their vibrant plumage and presence. We are co-creators, collaborating with Gaia, our ultimate muse, here to craft a harmonious existence.

Analytical approaches in modern education have overshadowed the role of art, restricting its presence to the 'professional' realm. Consumerism has further reduced art to a commodity measured solely by sales figures. To reclaim the essence of the expressive arts, we must shift our focus to the process and experience of creating, valuing the transformative journey of creativity over the final product or profitability. This emphasis on discovery aligns with the spiritual life, prioritising the journey rather than measurable outcomes or material gains.

The trope of the spiritual journey conveys a sense of constant movement and progression, never fully arriving, but always unfolding, discovering and (re)creating ourselves. Spirituality also involves a process of integrating different facets of our personality, experiences, and creative expressions. Engaging in the arts as a spiritual practice is honouring the process of meaning-making and cultivating a close relationship with mystery. It creates an openness inside us, a space to converse with God/Universal energy. When we become a clear channel for Source consciousness to speak to and through us, we learn to *listen*—not just through our ears but through our embodied senses—to the internal *nudges* and unanticipated 'ah-ha' moments.

INVITATION

Create something for the pure purpose of play!

Create a safe space where you feel confident to express yourself fully. Let go of the aspect of 'productivity' and of any expectation of what is 'good' or 'bad' in art, as there is no such thing. We are all artists and creatures of creation. It is one of our greatest gifts and a responsibility of life — to create in whichever way we choose. Our art is worthy of space and time.

Allow yourself to playfully create with no attachment to the outcome. Connect to your inner child, their childlike wonder will help you with this. If you are having trouble, think about what things brought you joy when you were young, and how you enjoyed expressing yourself creatively. As a child, you knew so well how to just have fun, be open and be present. Engage in what brought you joy back then, or some other way, maybe one that is completely new. Whether it's painting, dancing, writing poetry, cooking, sewing, growing a garden, growing a business, or some other enterprise, let yourself go, and flow without expectations.

Your finished creation may or may not become the basis of a commercial venture, or your life's purpose, but it will uncover inspiration. It may even uncover a lost part of yourself—one that has become suppressed and hidden—or uncover a newly found joy. Play will give you and your life more energy, as well as fuel your overall creativity, in all areas of life, including your career, home, and self-expression.

Use your creativity for the purpose of expressing your emotions. It can be hard to express how we feel through our voice or actions, but if you feel you have something to express, or something weighs heavy on your heart, use this energy to fuel your creativity. Let it go through the process, see what flows forth from your consciousness — write, paint, sculpt, sing, upcycle, cook, garden, photograph. Let it inspire you! If you need some extra inspiration ... look to Mother Nature, our greatest muse.

We all have a little artist inside that wants to play, and the whispering winds of air are reminding you that as you connect with your inner child in this playful way, you will be relieved of some stresses of your daily adult life.

Earth is our playground, and we must play forever. When we open ourselves up to the creative energy within, we are bringing new life into the world. Give birth to your ideas, let them manifest in the world!

15. Forgiveness
Let go, and forgive. It's time to move on.

CARD WISDOM

A Hawai'ian proverb states, "Before the sun goes down, forgive." For the *Kānaka Maoli* people of Hawai'i, non-violence is at the very heart of their community-based culture. Their ethos derives from gentleness, solidarity, and an extensive ecological reverence for all life, known in their language as *laulima*, translating literally as 'many hands'. It is the practice of the aloha spirit where the locals connect spiritually together and to the *'āina*—their land.

Native Hawai'ians follow a tradition of forgiveness through a ceremonial practice called *ho'oponopono*, an ancient sacrament that embodies the power of love in action. This practice involves a process of rectifying any wrongdoing in your relationships, whether it is with others, ancestors, deities, the earth, or even yourself. The primary aim of *ho'oponopono* is to restore peace and harmony, thereby facilitating healing from past traumas or violence and enabling the release of pain. It emphasises the significance of taking responsibility, showing respect and love, and seeking forgiveness and reconciliation. At its core, this practice is rooted in unity — a profound connection that binds us to everything and everyone, unbreakable and all-encompassing.

Earth is simply a school for our souls to explore the pursuit of growing in awareness, throughout our human life. Forgiveness plays a crucial role in this process, allowing us and others to make mistakes and learn from them, thus evolving into better versions of ourselves. When we hold on to past mistakes, replaying them over and over again in our minds, we struggle to move forward and accept ourselves. Forgiveness and freedom go hand in hand. By unconditionally forgiving ourselves and others, we embrace our shared humanity and recognise that everyone is doing their best, based on their knowledge, experiences, and unique perspective. We continually grow and evolve, leaving behind old versions of ourselves to become better. We are not the same person we were a year ago, or even five minutes ago. Mistakes are necessary for us to learn who we don't want to be and who we want to become. Rather than holding on to pain of the past, we should thank our past selves for guiding us towards growth. This awareness helps us to see others completely and to forgive them when we are met with a sincere apology.

INVITATION

Forgive yourself or another, now, in order to heal the situation. Holding on to resentment or unforgiving thoughts only drains your mind and body, weighing you down with unnecessary burdens. Forgiveness does not mean, "the pain you caused me is okay". It simply means, "I am no longer prepared to carry around pain in response to your actions". By holding on to grudges, we only punish ourselves in the process of our irritations and prolong the suffering. Partake in this beautiful practice of *ho'oponopono* by simply asking openly for forgiveness using a prayer that uses the four forces of repentance, gratitude, forgiveness, and love. These forces are reflected in the four phrases that make up this prayer, repeated in any order, silently to oneself, or out loud:

I am sorry. Please forgive me. I love you. Thank you.

The element of air reminds you that the present moment is real. Free yourself from your past now as it no longer exists. Let the wind blow all your fears away, leaving you fresh to begin anew in the now. Allow yourself to move forwards and expand into who you want to become, without allowing the memory of who you were yesterday to hold you back. Forgive yourself for anything that hasn't felt right, from your highest frequency of being. You are allowed to make mistakes. Making mistakes is part of being human and how we learn and rise. Be gentle on yourself; don't beat yourself up. Breathe into the present and breathe out your past. Your past self is so proud of who you are becoming!

Radiate this new, loving energy, come back to love, give thanks to your lessons, express trust, and let go.

All is forgiven.

16. Freedom

Don't be so hard on yourself. Free yourself from judgements and expectations — whether they are yours or others'.

CARD WISDOM

If we look at the people in our circle and we don't feel inspired, then we don't have a circle, we have a cage.

Criticism from others—but equally that of ourselves—can make us feel like a bird trapped in a cage. We feel trapped in our mind, not living free to be what we want to be, believing that we do not have the wings and the capability to fly high. We mustn't let our wings be clipped by criticism. Criticism is only a reflection and a projection of someone's own insecurities and problems, or a form of our own limiting beliefs.

When it comes to withstanding criticism projected onto us from others, like a torrential force of wind, we try to block it. To shelter a patio from the wind, we build a wall. Just like ourselves, when we defend against criticism, we put up a defensive inner wall to try and block an external attack. We shut down and turn to stone. But what happens when we turn to stone? We go cold, shut ourselves off, and end up caging the turmoil within us.

Trees, however, when obstructed by a huge hailstorm, do not place a barrier up before themselves. Instead, they stay strong, calm, and grounded, allowing the wind's obstruction to blow right through them. Their branches can bend in a hurricane, when a rigid structure, like a building, would come crashing down. It is the same with our emotions; if we are rigid when struck by an emotional storm, we are more likely to crumble from the impact. Trees can teach us about using non-violence and how we can respond to powerful forces without becoming violent in return. If we learn from trees and, instead, transform the energy coming at us—by staying grounded, listening rather than reacting, by swaying with the wind—we can then let the chaos blow itself out.

INVITATION

In this card, we see an image of an open bird cage, representing the feeling of being trapped, whether that is in a relationship, a job, or a situation. The open door signifies you are, by all means, free to fly away of your own accord — but something is keeping you on the edge.

The element of air is asking you to re-evaluate your commitments and what may keep you stuck and unable to live your best. Start by creating a list of your obligations and evaluate each one individually. Ask yourself if they still serve a purpose in your life and contribute positively to your growth and happiness. Identify any duties that may hold you back or prevent you from living the life you love or hindering your own self-love.

It is time to fly away from this negativity, from the situations and the people whom you have outgrown. When criticism comes your way like a fierce wind, instead of building walls to block it, let it pass through you like a gentle breeze. Just as you would not shelter a patio with a solid wall, do not shut yourself off from the world when faced with criticism. Turning to stone may offer temporary protection, but it also traps the turmoil within you, leaving you cold and disconnected.

Instead, embrace the liberation of being a free bird. Walk away from the restrictions that hold you back and release any fear of falling in flight. Dare to live dangerously free, rather than existing in a state of silent slavery to a mediocre life. Be unafraid of what others may say or think, breaking free from the cage you have created for yourself. Set boundaries that honour your true desires and be strong in expressing your authentic self.

Just as the wind carries both harsh gusts and gentle whispers, criticism may come in various forms. Allow it to pass by without taking it to heart, for your worth and purpose are not defined by others' judgements. Trust in your own journey, guided by your soul's purpose, and soar above the negativity. Embrace the power of your words — not to defend against criticism, but to affirm your own truth and create a life that aligns with your deepest aspirations. Embody the essence of a free bird, gracefully navigating the currents of life, unburdened by the weight of others' opinions.

Remember, freedom is not a place — it is a state of being. We have the power to free ourselves at any given moment. Set yourself free! The door to your dreams is wide open ...

Inspiration
Fresh inspirational ideas are fluttering your way.

17. Inspiration
Fresh inspirational ideas are fluttering your way.

CARD WISDOM

The element of air is associated with the rising sun in the east, the origin of new ideas, inspiration, and enlightenment. Air reflects thought and mind, intellect and reason, and is the breath of the Goddess, of Gaia and her living inspiration.

Breathing is a natural way to the heart. It is our vital lifeforce, energy that pulsates through our whole being. Within Hindu texts, the winds that circulate through our bodies are known as *vayus*, the connecting links between the material world, consciousness, and the mind. They involve a cycle of 'aspiration' (to breathe towards Great Spirit, to ascend, to soar) and 'inspiration' (to draw in, be in-filled with loving lifeforce energy, divinely inspired). These vital powers bring life to our bodies, exciting our impulses, emotions, and desires. The word 'inspiration' derives from the words 'to inspire' and 'breathe'. 'A breath of fresh air' suggests refreshing ideas, or an inspiring new approach to something.

Sylphs are spiritual creatures, associated with the element of air. They are shape-shifting, fae-like beings that travel through the air, surfing the winds and wild weather patterns. Practitioners of Wicca and other pagan practices usually invoke them in rites, rituals, or spells regarding the element of air or wind. They manifest themselves as certain cloud shapes in the sky. Sylphs are intermediaries between humans and higher realms of consciousness or divinity. By connecting with them, we may deepen our spiritual practice or gain new insights into our nature and purpose. Sylphs can also inspire and enhance creativity, helping us to tap into new sources of inspiration or find new ways to express our ideas and imagination.

Like winds, clouds, and fairies, thoughts come and go. But we can quieten the mind to an enlightened stillness; then it resembles a still, infinite sky. When interested, sylphs relate well with people whose minds have been disciplined through meditation. They also relate well with artists, in particular musicians and poets, as music and poetry flow like the wind.

INVITATION

You are about to receive a great deal of fresh inspiration. This will bring about a change in your life regarding how to pursue things further. You might find yourself down a new rabbit hole of research, opening up your world to new enlightening perspectives. Don't be afraid to jump down the hole — you are being encouraged to dive headfirst. You may get lost and feel a little windswept within this new knowledge, but it will eventually make sense and guide you in a way that inspires you and others.

If you have been experiencing some brain fog, or are an artist experiencing a creative block, unlock your creativity with this simple meditation:

Find a quiet space and close your eyes.

Take a moment to imagine a serene room within your mind. See this room as a metaphor for your creative space, a place where ideas flow freely and inspiration is abundant. Picture it filled with natural light, creating a sense of purity and clarity.

Take deep breaths, releasing any mental clutter or distractions out of a window in your inner room.

Shift your focus inward, embracing a state of inward stillness. With a calm mind, invite creative thoughts and ideas to enter your awareness.

Stay in this space for however long you like ...

... Then, whenever you are ready, gradually bring your focus back to your body, allowing yourself to journal and explore whatever inspiration arises.

Remember that you can return to this state and place whenever you desire to tap into your creative flow.

By clearing your mind through meditation, you will make room for fresh, universal inspiration to flutter through to you. It will be exactly what you need — even better than anything you can currently comprehend. If you are mid-creation and experiencing a block, give yourself permission to also take some time off from this endeavour. Hit the pause button on this project until you feel inspired once more.

You may also benefit from 'stream of consciousness' writing, which is a practice involving writing without forethought, ignoring punctuation, style, and grammar and simply letting your mind wander without stopping. Write for as long as you want to, until you feel a sense of completion. Alternatively, you can set a timer for just 10, 15, or 20 minutes, or set yourself a task to complete a set number of pages, then stop. This exercise can lead to great shifts, great insights, fresh inspiration, and a great sense of release. It allows room for you to gain inspiring insights into yourself and your world you may not otherwise have had. It also helps to articulate, and come to terms with, those thoughts and feelings that might keep you stuck.

You must guide your life with your inspiration at the forefront. From this point of direction, everything you create is from a place of intentional enjoyment. Avoid the trap of doubting your ideas, or thinking that they are too 'out there'. Your inspiration comes directly from the universal, creative source. Do not doubt the intelligence behind your ideas and creative urges.

18. Imagination

Give yourself permission to daydream. Your imagination is the portal to manifesting the life you desire.

CARD WISDOM

Our imagination is the portal extending beyond our mind and our immediate physical realm into the expansive field of interconnected energy that is always around us. It is the place where we can enter intergalactic, visionary worlds beyond our usual self and our limited 3D vision of the earth. Imagination takes us into the unlimited, etheric field of potentiality.

Sadly, many modern-day cultures do not value imagination, only deeming it acceptable as 'child's play' for our early years. When we are young our imagination is wild, free, and magical, everything is possible and there are no limitations to what we are capable of. As we become older, we must revert, principally, to a rational mindset. We are told to get our heads "out of the clouds", only believe in facts and figures, and act sensibly and responsibly, instead of "wasting time" by drifting off into daydreams. As a result, some joylessly lose touch with their imagination and their inner child entirely when advancing into adulthood. When we lose touch with our imagination, we limit our own experiences and the ways we can view the world. We cut ourselves off from the enchantment that fuels our creativity, meanwhile shutting ourselves off from creating the life we dream of.

But life wouldn't be what it is today without the writers, the poets, the inventors, innovators, and creatives. It is the dreamers who have transformed the imaginable into the tangible, by quite literally dreaming the unimaginable into existence. In 1865, Jules Verne's novel *From the Earth to the Moon* envisioned space travel and a moon landing, which became a reality in 1969 with the Apollo 11 mission. Isaac Asimov's 1951 short story *The Fun They Had* imagined a future with computers in every home and electronic learning. Allen Ginsberg's 1956 poem *America* expressed a vision of a society with technological advancements that have materialised today, such as smartphones, the internet, and social media platforms.

These pioneers of the visionary world transcended the limits of imagination. They fearlessly stepped outside the confines of the conventional thinking of their times and forged a path that led to remarkable advancements and transformative changes in our society. In doing so, they not only revolutionised our world, but also enriched our lives by revealing the infinite potential and profound power of human imagination.

INVITATION

This card tells you that your imagination, and the use of intentional visualisation, are powerful tools for manifesting when used together. Now is the time for you to make use of your innate skills.

Your energy is aligned with pure potential. It is important to know that everything you focus on now will expand in line with the energy field of whatever you put your mind and attention to.

Refine your desires and release any resistance and fears that hinder your progress. Draw these dreams into your reality like a magnet, by vividly envisioning their fulfilment every day, crafting a detailed blueprint for manifestation. Harmonise your energy with the universe, allowing your visualisations to act as a conduit, bringing your desires to vibrant life. Do this by visualising and feeling what it would be like to have what you want, right now. What does success or your ideal life look like to you? What would it feel like to achieve your biggest goals and aspirations? Imagine yourself living a life aligned with your values and purpose. Imagine the sensation of stepping your soul into your future self that already possesses it. Meditate on this; let your mind float heavenwards, up and past the clouds; float upwards yet inwards through your inner space of cosmic consciousness.

Your thoughts create. Strengthen the process by shifting your total energy towards how your body will feel with what you want, like it has already arrived. When you do this, the universe matches your frequency and the frequency of your desire — it magnetises it towards you.

Vision boards are a fun and powerful way to achieve clarity and focus about what you want to create. Place the vision board somewhere in your home where you will see it often. Every time you pass by and gaze at it, let yourself feel the excitement of how it would feel to have these aspects in your life. When we look around us with excited expectations of what we desire, we create space in our lives to bring them into reality.

19. Magic
There is magic in the air! Follow the signs.

CARD WISDOM

We could call magic 'thaumaturgical non-mechanistic psychology', but that term lacks the same ring to it. Experiencing magic, in the sense of miracles and real-life miraculous encounters, is a discipline of the mind. The journey starts by acquiring an initial comprehension of how consciousness is moulded. Our perception of reality is both constructed and constricted within the framework of the world we are raised to accept as 'known'.

People are so quick to dismiss the unseen, yet we live in a world where it is proven that we cannot see all the colours, smell all the smells, feel all the vibrations, or experience all that exists through our restrictive five senses alone. Fear of the unknown can keep us in denial of any aspects of magic. It is natural to discredit what the mind can't decipher and to destroy what we do not understand. The study of quantum physics has already laid down the groundwork for embracing the power of the unseen by providing an understanding of how the invisible world creates the visible world. The observer-effect hypothesis implies that the act of observing the invisible world can have a direct impact on its manifestation in the visible world, which may highlight the fundamental role of consciousness in shaping reality.

Earth magic and universal guidance is readily available to everyone, they just have to be nurtured and developed. Those with open consciousness and an open heart connected to their centre rise to realise the way life really works. They bond with the flow of energy, information, and intelligence all around us. They open themselves up to the underlying field of infinite potential present in our universe.

Many cultures revere ravens as a notable totem animal for magic. Their black colour symbolises the void from which all things originated, and to which all things will return. These birds are important messengers, able to cross time and space. Magic is a practice that allows us to work with the subtle aspects of energy and quantum forces to bring about changes in reality. It is the mystery that lies in the secret soul of the world, at the core of creation. What we imagine, we have the power to create.

INVITATION

Drawing this card is a sign that Great Spirit is trying to intervene and connect with you. It is asking you to keep all your senses active and open and be extra alert to see the synchronistic events, signs, symbols, and omens given to you through the oracle of the ordinary world.

Become more attuned to the natural world and you'll find that you experience signs more frequently. They tend to reoccur in a similar, personal manner; maybe for you it's through repeating numbers, visits by power animals, seeing feathers, or something else unique that you notice as a recurring, serendipitous circumstance. The essence of the air element wants to assure you that these messages and signs are not just coincidences. They are meant for you to see and use, to help you interpret what is going on in your realm. If you see repeated animals or signs, take note. Research their deeper meaning. What do the messages tell you? Connect to the power of these omens.

If you are unsure of the message, rest assured it will all become clear in good time. The universe likes to leave breadcrumbs for our curiosity. It may also just be a nudge from Great Spirit trying to grab your attention. What are you doing when this omen appears? What could be the alert message?

Your spirit guardians are always listening to your wishes and the whispers voiced to them. They are also willing to connect in the way that you want them to — you just have to ask. Take time today to quieten yourself. Ask a question to your spirit guides for direction; ask for a specific sign you wish to find so they can connect clearly with you. Maybe you ask to see the numbers '222' twice today, or to see a dove symbol, or some other object or icon. Make sure to be very specific, and don't be afraid to be creative or random. The universe always finds its way.

20. Transformation

**The struggle is nearly over. Your wings are on their way.
Get ready to soar!**

CARD WISDOM

There is no question that the process of metamorphosis is a miraculous ordeal. Let's just consider for a moment the kind of energy spent by our beautiful, winged friend, the butterfly ... Now, imagine the entirety of your life changing to such an extreme that you are unrecognisable at the end of the transformation. This is her deepest symbolic lesson — for the butterfly is the notable totem for transformation. With ease and grace, she embraces the changes required of her body and of her environment — from egg, to caterpillar, to cocooning in her chrysalis, to finally unfurling into her majesty, wearing her finest winged gown. This deep acceptance of her metamorphosis is such a strong symbolism of her faith, from cocoon to a crown jewel.

The fascinating life of the butterfly closely mirrors our process of spiritual transformation. We each have the opportunity to be reborn by going within. By withdrawing from the world into our inner being, surrounding ourselves in cocoons of prayer, self-care, meditation, or contemplation, we're ready, at some point, to emerge. Awakened and ready to fly, we transform ourselves and rebirth into an entirely new way of being.

The movement of our own deep, profound transformation is a mythical one. It takes the collapse and abandonment of an old understanding, as well as the destruction of an old narrative, to grow into a new one. Struggle is a natural part of the butterfly's growth process. The emergence from their cocoon serves a crucial purpose in ensuring the proper development and strengthening of their wings for flight. This demonstrates that, even in our most difficult days, we are only gaining more strength. It is all divine warriors' work to burst through the battle and break free, into the next phase of being. We must never forget that we will always, eventually, break through to see more light.

INVITATION

This card signifies you are at the end of a phase in your life which has served its purpose. Just like a butterfly emerging from its cocoon, you are about to break through a current stage of cocooning. Perhaps you have been feeling closed off or in need of more rest. You are now ready to transition into a spacious and exciting new evolutionary stage of your life.

You are flying away from stagnancy and breaking free from feeling held back, moving into a more purposeful phase. Do not be concerned about endings; they are bringing in the new for you, which is aligned much more with the current version of yourself.

You may feel open, bare, and vulnerable, as your energetic field is being stripped of anything that is no longer serving you, as well as feeling pulled from your cocooning comfort blanket. But please know that you are being cared for physically, mentally, and emotionally by the Great Spirit. This may be why you feel especially emotional, or overwhelmed by your feelings. Be assured that this is to enable the process of your own transformation to take place. Honour your feelings and allow yourself to feel them, but then smile, knowing that even better things are on their way to you. Hold this faithful trust in greater intelligence, for it knows what you want and need, better than you know yourself.

You may find it beneficial to engage in a symbolic act of creating a visual representation or artwork that represents the phase you are letting go of, and ceremoniously releasing it, by burning it and offering its ashes in the wind. This can serve as a physical reminder of your transformation and help you embrace the new phase of being that awaits you.

The combined presence of the air element and your guides envelops you in a cocoon of support and inspiration. Feel their nurturing embrace as you prepare to soar towards the light! There is so much more freedom and excitement awaiting you. Break free and open your wings!

The Golden Key of Fire

The *Golden Key of Fire*, the element of the south, radiant in its essence, holds the transformative power to ignite the dormant flames within our being. It unlocks our inner passion and vitality, infusing us with the courage to embrace change and take bold action.

Fire sparks the flames of creativity, urging us to express our authentic selves and unleash our hidden potential. Like a blazing inferno, fire illuminates the path of self-discovery, guiding us towards our genuine desires and purpose. It purges and purifies, burning away the limitations and fears that hinder our growth. Just as a phoenix rises from the ashes, fire teaches us the art of transformation and resilience, reminding us that even in the face of adversity, we can be reborn with greater strength and determination. With the *Golden Key of Fire*, we can harness its transformative energy to bring warmth, illumination, and empowerment into our lives and the lives of others.

21. Flame of Passion
Dance to the beat of your own heart, and love will follow.

CARD WISDOM

When we speak of being 'on fire', it generally implies an intense enthusiasm for something. Just like when we are feeling 'on a roll', we feel ignited by being passionately immersed in the activity we are doing.

Often associated with intimacy and lovemaking, passion is a fiery and fierce energy that illuminates our inner being and motivates action. Just like being in the arms of a divine lover, passion can be both exhilarating and overwhelming. In those fleeting moments, the intensity of love's fervour can leave its mark, be it through a passionate bite or a forceful grip. Yet, within such embraces lies a yearning for more life — a begging for more of this burning love, rather than a plea for it to cease. This passionate force can manifest in our everyday lives when we relinquish judgements of right/wrong or spiritual/mundane, unveiling ourselves to the extent that only love remains. There is no opposition, even when confronted with unforeseen challenges and the bruises inflicted by life's circumstances — the Divine only intends to seduce. Embracing this truth grants us permission to wholeheartedly love what we love, live as we wish, and liberate ourselves entirely from the confines of conventional expectations, regardless of whether or not they make sense to others. We were not born to explain ourselves or make sense to anyone else.

When the fires of passion burn bright within us, the rhythm of our heartbeats and the heartbeat of Mother Earth merge. It reminds us how we interconnect with one another and all of creation. As we synchronise our bodies to this primal rhythm, we become part of a universal concert of creation, where free movement becomes the essential element, like a dance. While our modern society often imposes restrictions on us, dictating how we should move and behave, it is crucial to remember that each of us possesses a unique rhythm within our hearts. It is our soul responsibility, our duty, to dance to that rhythm. By attentively listening and harmonising with the background music of Mother Earth, we can reclaim our innate freedom. We must not allow external validations to crash our own party and hinder us from dancing around the fire of our hearts, to the beat of our soul's song. Life is a cosmic dance between our souls and the Source, and passion serves as its enchanting soundtrack. The Divine extends an invitation, asking for your hand — will you take this dance?

INVITATION

This is an invitation to find lost parts of yourself — perhaps your sensual aspects or the capacity to deeply admire yourself. Romanticise your life with, and for, yourself. If you are calling in a partner, stop frantically searching. Give all the love you have to yourself first. Whether you have a partner or not, use time now to discover yourself, and your own passions. Fill yourself with love. Take yourself on a date, on an adventure. Dance with yourself, dress up for yourself. Leave kind notes in library books, smile a lot. Speak lovingly to yourself in the mirror and become your own divine lover. The relationships around you will reflect the love you have for yourself, as it ripples out of your emanating heart. You will start to magnetise the love you are destined to co-create in this lifetime.

For this soul work, dig deep into your heart centre. Seek out what passions lay dormant there, ones you may have unconsciously suppressed. These are the aspects of yourself that are yearning to be expressed once more. Maybe it's a part of yourself that used to love to paint, to dance, to sing, to write, or bake. Focus on your own joy and forget about comparing yourself to others. By indulging in the things that make your heart sing, you will naturally align with the rhythm of life, attracting like-minded people and experiences that fulfil your deepest desires. Let your passion be your guide, leading you towards a more fulfilling life.

22. Courage

Muster up the courage to act in accordance with your highest light.

CARD WISDOM

Lions, the kings of the animal kingdom, have long captivated the human imagination with their resounding roars and fearless nature. Their regal presence and courageous spirit serve as powerful inspiration, urging us to confront our deepest fears and embrace our own inner strength.

Tippi Degré, a modern Mowgli of our time, is a remarkable young girl who grew up in South Africa for the first 10 years of her life. She was raised by her parents who worked as wildlife photographers and filmmakers, as well as the wild animals that inhabited her homeland. She had a unique upbringing, roaming the wild landscape accompanied by her childhood companions: lions, elephants, and other untamed creatures. Tippi embodied the essence of Lion's courage, fearlessly forming a deep connection and understanding of the natural world, despite the inherent risks and challenges. Tippi bravely embraced the opportunity to learn from these creatures, forming bonds of trust and respect. She approached them with a sense of curiosity and wonder, recognising their innate beauty and the importance of coexistence. Tippi's courage enabled her to see beyond the surface-level perceptions of these animals as dangerous or threatening, allowing her to form lasting connections and friendships with them.

Her experiences with wild animals not only showcased her fearlessness, but also taught her valuable lessons about compassion, empathy, and the interconnectedness of all living beings. Tippi's story serves as a powerful reminder that courage lies in facing our fears, embracing the unknown, and finding common ground with that which is misunderstood or feared.

Tippi's story inspires us to approach life with bravery, open-mindedness, and a willingness to connect with the world around us, even in the face of uncertainty. It teaches us that true courage lies in embracing our differences, bridging divides, and fostering a deep appreciation for the beauty and wisdom that exist within the wild and untamed corners of our world.

INVITATION

You are being encouraged to gather up the courage to do something outside of your comfortable enclosure to act in alignment with your highest light. This may require you to change your behaviour, or break free from the patterns and habitual routines that have become comfortable to you. By doing so, you can align yourself with your deepest truth and pave the way for healing and growth.

Take a moment to reflect: Are you truly meeting your needs? Are you taking responsibility for your actions? Are you standing up for yourself and your truth? Are you aligning with universal love?

Courage isn't always about playing the hero — it presents itself in various forms daily. Courage looks like being your vulnerable self, just as you are, imperfections and all. Courage looks like taking responsibility for meeting your own needs. It looks like taking your opinion of yourself back from the grip of the opinions of others. It takes so much courage to stand up for what you know in your heart is right. Sometimes it even takes courage to take a nap!

Courage and openness go hand in hand. To explore new possibilities, you must break free from the confines of comfort and take risks. This is especially true when fear holds you captive, causing you to cling to familiar ways or stay fixated on only seeing and doing things one way, which is your own way.

During moments of frustration, it's tempting to lash out and react in ways misaligned with your highest light. However, remember that your true self—your core essence—is resilient and cannot be diminished. In moments of hurt, the desire to retaliate may arise, to inflict more pain upon those who have wounded you. Yet, such a mindset perpetuates a cycle of suffering, a snowball effect that engulfs one person after another. Instead, let mindfulness be your guide, setting aside the ego's demands, and approaching the situation with the courageous, compassionate heart of a hero. If you find yourself in this position, grasp the opportunity for growth and transformation that this challenge presents. Embrace the lesson with love, and channel any excess anger as a catalyst for positive change. Dance and shake off negativity, or even let loose a mighty roar from a hilltop. Let the energy flow through you, empowering yourself and those around you, fostering liberation instead of harm. Roar not in retaliation or anger, but as a symbol of your resilience and your freedom.

You don't require a shield of white light; you are the light and also the shadow. Courageously claim it.

23. Burning Desire

Align your burning desires with selflessness and higher purpose. The universe will reciprocate, bringing unimaginable fulfilment to your life.

CARD WISDOM

The flames flickering in someone's eyes as they passionately speak about their deepest desires and dreams. The electric surge of fiery energy coursing through our veins when we discuss our passions. These are the inner flames setting our souls ablaze with purpose and meaning. The light within guides us, beckoning us to follow its glow and illuminating the way to our dreams.

Within spiritual circles, there is a misconception that *all* desires inevitably lead to suffering, a misinterpretation of ancient spiritual truths. Desires, in and of themselves, are not inherently good or bad.

They are natural aspects of our human experience and can serve as powerful motivators for action and personal growth. However, it is crucial to understand that some desires can bind us, creating attachment and ultimately leading to suffering when we become overly fixated on their fulfilment or when they arise from egoic cravings.

To discern between 'pure desires' and 'egoic cravings' we must recognise that pure desires align with the code of conduct of all creation. They originate from a space of love, joy, and harmony, seeking the wellbeing of all. On the contrary, egoic cravings are driven by fear, anger, greed, loss, or other negative emotions, stemming from self-centeredness and disregarding the interconnectedness of all beings. When desires arise from egoic cravings, they go against the energy of love that permeates the universe. Examples of egoic craving include acting selfishly to fulfil personal desires without regard for the wellbeing of others, exploiting resources, or exploiting others' vulnerabilities for personal gain.

In the practice of *karma yoga*, desires are acknowledged and understood, but the focus shifts from personal gain to selfless service and the pursuit of the greater good of all. It involves transcending egoic wants and attachments and acting without seeking personal rewards or outcomes, with a deep sense of duty, dedication, and surrender to a higher purpose or the Divine. By aligning our desires with selflessness and embracing the path of *karma yoga*, we can find fulfilment and contribute positively to the world.

INVITATION

When you draw this card, reflect on your desires and their motivations. Are they driven purely by personal gain and gratification, or can you redirect them towards benefiting others and the greater good?

The elemental flames within you emphasise the importance of harmonising your personal desires with the desires of the universe. By aligning your intentions with selflessness and service, you create a powerful resonance that attracts opportunities and manifests your highest good.

Remain mindful of any egoic attachments and the potential for self-centred cravings. *Karma yoga* teaches us to release the need for personal gain and instead focus on the selfless intentions behind our actions. Use your talents and passions to benefit others. If your burning desire is to express yourself through art, you could use your artwork to inspire and uplift others, or perhaps donate your creations to charitable causes. By infusing your desires with a selfless intention, you expand the impact of your art beyond personal satisfaction.

Another example of selfless action is seeking personal success and abundance with the intention of sharing and giving back. If your burning desire is to achieve financial abundance, align your intention with using your resources to support those in need. By ensuring that you root your desires in the service others, you create a cycle of abundance and generosity.

Trust this process of allowing your desires to merge with universal desires. You will soon witness the magic that unfolds as it will create a powerful resonance that propels you forward. What you desire also desires you. All desires stem from an infinite intelligence, and you possess the potential to bring about positive changes in the world around you. Trust this process of allowing your desires to merge with the universal desires. You will soon witness the magic that unfolds. What you desire also desires you. Just as the acorn contains the mighty oak tree within it, your pure desires harbour the seeds of their own fulfilment.

24. Integrity

Align your actions with your inner values.
Be true to yourself and own up to any mistakes.

CARD WISDOM

The first use of fire is one of the most influential moments in modern human history. It is recorded right alongside tool making and art in the pages of anthropology textbooks. Humans, however, are not the only ones who can purposefully manipulate fire for their benefit.

The mythologies of some Australian First Nations mention the association between fire and birds. Different stories tell of a 'firehawk' — a bird that earned its name because of its notorious branch-burgling antics. The firehawk swipes branches from cooking fires, wildfires, or other mythical animals who hold fire. Some species of raptors have been seen in the wild carrying burning sticks to fresh locations, using the flames held in their beaks or talons to propagate fire in new areas to flush out prey. While advantageous for the firehawks, it can have devastating consequences for other life.

Like wildfire, the first spark of gossip is much the same. Conflict, misunderstandings, or disagreements set a spark, and the first whisper leaves behind a wisp of smoke. The smoke, when fanned into flame, spreads quickly, resulting in ruined relationships and combusted communities. The New Testament describes gossip as a wildfire:

> *Even so the tongue is a little member and boasts great things. See how great a forest a little fire kindles! And the tongue is a fire, a world of iniquity. The tongue is so set among our members that it defiles the whole body, and sets on fire the course of nature; and it is set on fire by hell.*
>
> —James 3:5–6 (NKJV)

Wildfires are driven by wind, much like gossip spreading from the force of 'winding someone up'. The fumes of fury thicken, causing harmful pollution to linger in the atmosphere. It doesn't take much to fan the flames of misinformation, but it takes a strong effort to put it out. Gossiping is not having integrity with yourself. Integrity is being aligned with what's right — especially when no one is looking. In integrity, we remain aligned with what is good and fair, because of our innate sense, not because someone told us. We are born with our higher sense of interconnection, of being good to others, which then reflects in being good to ourselves.

Integrity isn't a matter of opinion — it is awareness of the inner moral compass that guides us all. Happiness and loss of integrity are not synonymous. In truth, true happiness requires great integrity! We must not let our integrity slip in order to succeed, avoid conflict, or gain acceptance. These 'accidents' will only eat away at us, like mites. In moments like these we may seem to have misplaced our soul. Without it there is no way we can feel good about ourselves. Integrity is the gift that will bring us a powerful peace of mind and a loving self-respect. It is always important to stop and look at the decisions we have made and make choices which are more in alignment with our higher selves.

Yet, what a relief it is to know that our valued integrity is there deep within us, and that we can reconnect with it at a moment's notice.

INVITATION

To be in alignment with your highest integrity, be absolutely honest with yourself and completely honest with others. Honesty is the way to truly step into your magic. Allow your truth to fuel your inner fire — not to scold, but to heal. Let it radiate through your words, your actions, and your entire being. Honour your words and actions, by doing what you say you will do, when you say you will do it; by doing what is right, your power will rise. Your karma becomes clear. No matter what has gone on before, choosing honesty means that whatever is revealed is for your highest good. It will bring you freedom.

Your integrity towards your soul and your unique story will inspire others, even those who pretend not to see you. Never forget this: your authentic existence—guided by your own strength, and paving your own way—is infectious! It holds the power to spread and inspire others to do the same.

If there is conflict around you, don't lower yourself to that vibration by participating or acting in retaliation. Instead, take action of your own accord, walk away. Clear, ground, balance, and protect yourself. Protect your peace and protect others, by keeping the frequency of peace and love. Don't forget, people don't always remember what you say, but they always remember how you made them feel. Be integral in every way to your word, to your work and how you hold space for others. Leading with the highest vibration of love ensures you will sleep peacefully, knowing you acted in the highest good of yourself and all.

If you feel that you have made a mistake or have something that you need to take ownership of, be brave now in accepting and taking responsibility. Trust that your truth will always set you free! You are not your mistakes — mistakes are just happy accidents. You can begin again.

25. Shine Bright

Stop dimming your light to make others comfortable or for fear of being judged. Shine brighter!

CARD WISDOM

Within us, there is a light. Depending on where in our spiritual development we are, that light might be a flickering flame or a roaring bonfire. It's there, and if we stay consistent, tending to the flames, it will only shine brighter and mightier!

Spiritually, light captures the essence of our hearts and souls. Each entity and being contains Great Spirit's living flame—consciousness and aliveness—with its own right to be respected and honoured for its unique power and gift. A gift which we must all individually develop and bring forward, to become a beacon of bright light for one another, to guide each other like individual lighthouses back home to the harbour of our hearts. A lighthouse doesn't ask for permission to shine — it shines, tall and still, guiding those who need its light to safety.

As we release old, worn-out, limiting beliefs about ourselves and reach higher ways of being, we sometimes, somehow, fall right back into our humanness and create new ones. We hold back and worry that we aren't doing enough, or being enough, or that we're being too much for others, comparing ourselves to others and their achievements. We feel the need to hold ourselves back to protect us from rejection and judgement, but our spirit—just like a lighthouse and our Father Sun—does not stop shining out of fear of what others will think. It beams as bright as possible for all to see, feel, and be guided out from the darkness.

None of us have come as far as we have, through as much as we have and across the unknown, to stop here. We have not embarked on this journey to go backwards, returning to passivity and becoming the mildest and most toned-down version of ourselves. Our ancestors did not go through all that they did for us to stop and conform to societal norms that contradict our authentic selves, to fit into a mould that is familiar to others' eyes but foreign to our hearts.

We are beacons of beaming light, a fractal of a star, a part of the entire universe. We were born to shine our light, sharing our unique soul flame with the rest of the world.

INVITATION

You are at a stage in your awakening where you are levelling up and becoming something so much lighter and brighter. Do not dim your light to make others feel comfortable. You are composed of 15 trillion cells, all of which are rooting for you. So, stop acting small!

Sometimes, competition can emerge when you shine brightly in the world. If you feel attacked or looked down on when sharing your magic, remember that these people most likely want what you have. Do not let anyone stand in your way and shade your shine. If you have jealousy towards someone else, stop and reflect on why that is so — there is probably something in you that needs healing. There is no use in judging someone's life by comparing it to yours. Let other people's successes inspire you rather than frustrate you. If they can have it, so can you.

Consider the teachers, speakers, or role models who have influenced you the most. Chances are, you admire them because they are confident in expressing their ideas and values while embracing their individuality. Embody this same confidence and energy now — a rewarding new doorway of success may just open up for you by doing so. Share your wisdom and insights, and don't let self-doubt hold you back. Remember that your unique perspective is valuable and can make a significant impact.

You have been hiding in the shadows for too long. It is time to stop suppressing. Step out into the world and shine your beautiful light as bright as you can. You are a beautiful, loving, shining light on this planet and a powerful role model for others. Keep up the wonderful work and do not underestimate the power you express, simply by living your truth. You inspire people, far more than you are aware of.

The earth needs your light, and it can only come from you stepping fully into your power.

PS: You are never, ever 'too much'!

26. Be Brave

Choose to be a warrior, not a worrier. Your wounds are your war paint. You are much braver than you think.

CARD WISDOM

Over the centuries, our ancestors faced countless trials and tribulations, yet they met their challenges head on. From global wars to revolutions, deadly voyages and diseases; from witches being burned at the stake to living in and around harsh conditions — our descendants endured many challenges.

> *Your ancestors did not survive everything that nearly ended them for you to shrink yourself to make someone else comfortable. This sacrifice is your war cry, be loud, be everything and make them proud.*
>
> — Nikita Gill

It is the consequences of their brave fights and sacrifices that still light our way today. We are warriors, just like our ancestors — constantly transforming and stepping into our truths. And just like our ancestors, we are powerful, strong, courageous, and free, yet also vulnerably human. We are still sensitive, emotional, and loving beings. Even the mightiest of warriors still feel. It is integral to the human condition and came with the contract for our incarnation here, on this planet. We cannot run away from our feelings without them chasing us. This is why we should cherish and nurture the frailer aspects of ourselves.

Bravery and vulnerability are two sides of the same coin, equally important polarities. They are what make us who we are — as individuals, partners, parents, brothers, and sisters; as friends, and caregivers and takers; as compassionate listeners and as healers too. Being whole includes our holes. The *true* healers are the warriors who have been to war with the darkness inside, slayed their inner daemons, and emerged victorious, wearing their wounds as warpaint, ready to serve as spiritual sergeants.

The bravest heroic journey of all is the one that leads you back to you. We all have wounds, yet if we use them to power us forward, we win the battles that stand before us.

INVITATION

You are not a worrier, you are a warrior! You are brave and have the strength to win the fight you are facing. When you battle your inner daemons, be reassured that your army of angels have your back. They are here to remind you that your soul cannot be weakened or wounded; it's the one part of your being that always remains healed and whole. Spirit is always protecting you, so give your worries away now — they aren't yours to hold on to any longer. This card urges you not to define yourself by your wounds, but to heal them with love — it is your strongest sword. Experience how much energy and vitality you gain by slaying the sad stories that linger. Worrying means you suffer twice; it is a losing battle. You are here to win.

When you are holding on to old wounds you may notice they are all connected; rooted in one deep, primal, dark wound. However, it's time to leave the past behind and revolutionise yourself into a new state of being. Allow those old stories to wither, decay, and burn, as they have passed their expiration date and no longer serve a purpose. Feelings of unworthiness, fear of failure, guilt, regret — all these pains can easily be traced back to the desire for a perfect life. Be brave, let these stories go, and fight on with a new sense of freedom in your heart. Stand strong, hold your ground, and use your wounds as your warpaint to go on fighting to be better in the world.

Being brave isn't about being emotionless — the fire element also reminds you it's okay to *feel*. Honour your humanness. Allow yourself to process the emotions you have been experiencing through your time of transformation. Feel it to heal it. You've got this!

27. Phoenix Rising
Burn old personal paradigms that are keeping you stuck and rise into new ones.

CARD WISDOM

Existence is a series of cycles of life–death–life manifestations; an ever-cycling pattern permeating the universe and all existence, from the death and birth of stars to the ever-regenerative cycling of the seasons.

We experience this cycle on a macrocosmic level as well. It is through the cycles of life—birth, childhood, adolescence, parenthood, and our elder years—that we transcend each stage, shedding our previous identities and embracing new ways of relating to the world. We like to cling to the idea of permanence, holding on to it so tightly that every little unfortunate happening in our lives feels like a knock-out from which we might not get back up. We miss the acceptance and surrender to the process of our path's unfolding. Letting go of our rigid fixation on things going our way, we trust the way of the universe, embracing this life–death–life cycle as part of natural growth. We are continuously growing, shedding, and changing internally and externally. We are moving in different directions, just like the planets and stars, whirling through the sky. We die and are reborn, time and time again, in this one lifetime. It is our evolution that makes us stronger.

In the West, the alchemical symbol of the phoenix represents this truth. This mythical bird with vibrant red, orange, and gold feathers is believed to rise from its own ashes, signifying the triumph over death and the transcendent nature of the human spirit. It represents the stages of the alchemical process: the dissolution of the old, the purification of the self, and the emergence of a renewed and enlightened state of being. This spiritual symbolism reminds us of the inherent potential for transformation and the continuous cycle of life, death, and rebirth. It invites us to embrace our own journey of self-discovery, knowing that we can rise from the ashes of our hardships and embody our highest spiritual potential. As Clarissa Pinkola Estés expressed so eloquently, in her timeless book, Women Who Run with the Wolves:

> *Sometimes the one who is running from the Life/Death/Life nature insists on thinking of love as a boon only. Yet love in its fullest form is a series of deaths and rebirths. We let go of one phase, one aspect of love, and enter another. Passion dies and is brought back. Pain is chased away and surfaces another time. To love means to embrace and at the same time to withstand many endings, and many many beginnings- all in the same relationship.*

INVITATION

This card signals the end of a cycle within you, or a relationship, job, project, or a way of being. You may have a desire to declutter and get rid of old possessions that no longer resonate with the person you are now. Energetically burn or cut the ties you have to that which no longer serves your soul, as they will only hold you from rising into your full phoenix form.

We tend to cling to things. Clinging is only an attachment that will leave no room for new and better things. Letting go will allow space for the new to fit into its rightful place, and to sit comfortably within this current version of you. This also means letting go of opinions, doubts, despair, and fears. Clinging to your own limiting beliefs could be what's holding you back from rising towards the light of positivity and growth. Allow the flame within your heart to engulf you. Embrace the transformative power of alchemy and transmute the base metal of your doubts and fears into the golden essence of possibility. See that nothing truly dies, but instead changes from one ending, directly into new beginnings. Burn with love, for love.

You are the phoenix, yet again rising out of the ashes of outdated versions of yourself, becoming a brighter light here on Earth. You are ready to regenerate yourself in a more authentic way — a way that leads you back to who you truly are and helps you to recognise why you came here.

Time to level up!

28. Rekindle

Rekindle burnt out relationships by igniting them with more love.

CARD WISDOM

Fire was a giant springboard for mankind from the first time the early humans (known as 'Homo erectus') could create it. It changed our livelihood as a species exponentially, through our capacity to generate heat and light. Fire made it possible to cook food, to stay warm in cooler climates, and keep predators away at night.

Aside from it adding more comfort and convenience to our lives as a species, it also brought with it increased conversation with its power to bring people and communities closer together. Gathering by firelight was an ingrained, primal experience, when all we had was each other. Within the darkness, the light from a fire was a place to feast and tell stories. This is why we innately associate a shared fire with kinship and security — we feel a little more 'at home' with others. Rapport seems to come easier, and in one way or another we have an urge to talk to those that we rarely talk to. Sometimes we even break out in song! With a show of dancing fire flames adding to the already impressive atmosphere.

Throughout history, women have gathered in sisterhood, coming together in sacred circles or around ceremonial altars. In prehistoric times, they would sit around a fire connecting with the ancient traditions. One such tradition was the 'red tent', a ritual space symbolising Mother Earth's womb, where women would gather on the new moon to honour the sacred time of menstruation. Women have gathered in the secretive monasteries of the Middle Ages, in the consciousness-raising groups of the 1970s, and now, in modern era, these gatherings occur in more public places, even on online platforms. Women have long congregated to celebrate the secrets of the sister spirit — to laugh, share, heal, care for children, grieve, and spiritually connect in their communities. Within the structure of the circle, we harness a collective power. There is no hierarchy; each woman's voice is equally important; her story and history are honoured and fully received by others. When we create a sacred container with a primary focus on intention and healing, remarkable magic unfolds, benefiting both individuals and the collective.

These traditions live on today. The power of the internet enables like minds from all over the world to connect in this manner with easy access. More men these days are also communing together in sacred brotherhood, though it is not within the 'normal' culture of today's world for men to gather in this way. The feminine qualities of interconnection, vulnerability, relatedness, and cooperation are particularly undervalued in a masculine, patriarchal society, which instead celebrates individuality, dominance, and competition. But we cannot forget the greatness of vulnerability as a species and the immeasurable power of people gathering to hold each other's hearts in solidarity. We are all sisters and brothers on this singular planet we call home. We must all do the inner work to clear our ancestral wounds and shape a better world for our children.

INVITATION

Rekindle any relationships that have lost their spark by tending to them with more love, putting more intentional effort in. Can you be more present with the people around you? Energy is everything in relationships. Even the subtleness of presence can be felt strongly by others, making them feel fully seen and heard, and tightening the bond between you. Spend less time on your phone or being semi-distracted in conversation, and spend more time being *fully present*. Share more stories and get to know others who are just outside your circle. Be with them on a deeper level, rather than just from a simple, surface conversational level. You may find you have something to learn from them or you end up becoming great friends.

If you find that there are loose ends in your relationships, it's beneficial to take steps towards reconciliation by tying them up with forgiveness. This can involve letting go of old grudges or resentments that may be holding the relationship back and creating stagnation. Give thanks for the lessons that the other person has taught you, even if those lessons were hard to learn. Recognising the value of those experiences can help to foster a sense of grace and appreciation for the role that the other person has played in your life journey. Taking this step can help to release any negative energy and create space for growth and positive change.

29. Mask Off

You don't need to suppress to impress by hiding parts of yourself. Take off any masks to reveal the real you.

CARD WISDOM

The Toltec came to prominence in central Mexico a little over a millennia ago. Influenced by the Mayans, the Toltecs were a cultured society, who would later inspire the Aztecs. According to their traditions, we often adopt temporary masks and identities in our interactions, as if borrowing them for a fleeting moment, to engage with each other in a particular way. For instance, today we may borrow a mask to play the role of a mother and wife; but tomorrow a writer, teacher, runner, or even a football fan, wearing a mask to show how we relate to each other in specific social contexts. Mastery of self is to know that none of these masks are our true nature. A mask is simply knowledge formed by the agreements we use to interact with life, with people — a mask is an identity. When we live this roleplay unconsciously, we believe that who we are is the mask; but when we drop the facade from our face, we no longer hide who we are. Interactions are momentary agreements our bond has created, and this has shaped the way we see each other and ourselves.

Among pre-Columbian Mesoamerican cultures, such as the ancient Aztecs and Mayans, masks portrayed quite the opposite — they were worn in their rituals or carnivals and in their sacred dances as a metaphor. The mask was taken on and worn as a representation of the inner spiritual being, putting outward that which only lives inward. They understood that there is no human mask to hide behind, only the gesture and freedom to connect to the inner spirit. So, the mask was worn to show their connection to their inner being, while covering the face of the human mask.

When we drop our masks, we tell others we are no longer willing to play a role that they know and love. This role may be that of a mother, worker, or even a certain social status or personality trait, all of which come with expectations to maintain certain appearances. We are multifaceted beings that defy categorisation and cannot be labelled, uniformed, and put neatly into a box. By trying to fit into a narrow stereotype, we suppress the allowance of all parts of ourselves. For example, a punk rock bartender can be an avid flower painter, revealing both their edgy and gentle sides; a super glamorous girly-girl can also enjoy video games, expressing their love for adventure and fantasy; a mother can still be sensual and fun, and an influential politician who is an accomplished skateboarder, breaking stereotypes by being both a leader and a rebel in their personal life. We should not fear judgement for deviating from social norms, as we are not stereotyped 'roles' to perform, we are like diamonds, with many faces and facets. When we hide or suppress parts of ourselves, we risk losing touch with our true nature, becoming a hidden gem that nobody can see. Embracing all aspects of ourselves, we let our unique brilliance shine through. By doing so, we gain a crystal-clear vision of who we are, what the world has to offer, and what we offer the world, allowing us to explore its full spectrum of possibilities with confidence and authenticity.

INVITATION

In this moment, look closely at yourself and identify the masks you are hiding behind. It is time to gently drop them and show the world your entire self.

You may find you try to become someone you're not to impress others. You may exaggerate a story, adding a few dramatic details to make you more appealing. The real person becomes hidden behind a persona worn as a mask of deception. Maybe you're hoping to control a situation, or perhaps to mask the part(s) of you that feel vulnerable, afraid, or inadequate. When you come home from work, when the show is over, it's time to take off your masks and become your true self again. Sometimes you become fixated on wearing a mask; but just like wearing a physical mask, it's hard to breathe. If you practise wearing this mask for too long, it will imprison who you truly are.

Are you changing yourself to mould into an ideal image that fits with someone else's judgement? When we become tangled between what other people want and what they think is best for us, we lose ourselves. We play roles and put on a show to please others. Remember, it is not their life to live — this is your show. Let go of any expectations and visions of who others want you to be or what they want you to achieve. Who do *you* want to be? What do you want to do with *your* time here, and put *your* precious energy into? Own your opinion of yourself, it is the only opinion that truly matters. Take off any costumes hiding the real you and feel empowered to show up exactly as you are, because you are perfect, exactly as you are.

Take off any victim-hoods and remove the masks you are wearing as they shade your energy. Do not waste your energy in trying to play a role, just to please your ego. Just be a witness, observe if the ego role is being played out by others. Stay integral with *your* truth.

30. Burnout

Slow down. You don't want to burn things out or burn yourself out.

CARD WISDOM

As a culture, we hold high expectations of ourselves to be the same every day—to look after our families, go to work, be fit, be productive, race around and get things done—but we're not the same every day. Some days we're bursting with energy, others we are not. Some days we want to be sociable and surround ourselves with people, other days we'd rather be alone at home, surrounded by blankets and snacks. We often want it all and to be perfect, putting ourselves on pedestals, hoping to be the perfect parent, partner, or friend. We want to be seen as doing the perfect job, keeping fit, keeping up on trends, keeping up online, keeping up our appearances, and doing all the other things we need to do to have a 'perfect life'. But our expectations, and this need to be 'perfect', can drive us straight towards burnout.

Remembering our sacred relationship with the natural cycles of life and the changing seasons awakens our innate sensory-body wisdom. This intuitive wisdom empowers us to become our own healer and guide, guiding us towards a deeper understanding of our own cycles. As we observe the seasonal cycles, we learn about the various phases within us: the creative, manifesting energy of spring; the summery periods of expansiveness, fruition, and increased energy; the autumnal times when we need to release and let go of who, and whatever, must pass; the wintry phases when life slows down, resting before the new seeds of intention are planted, ready for the fresh spring. Women, in particular feel these phases over the lunar or menstrual month.

As we start to read and respond to the subtle signals of these cycles, we develop a relationship with our body's natural rhythm, and balance naturally follows. We begin to feel more at peace with our fluctuating emotions and gain a heightened understanding of when we are our most creative, tired, playful, or sensitive selves. This enables us to honour our and our body's multifaceted moods without resisting or battling against ourselves. We no longer suppress our emotions, push ourselves too far, or grow frustrated with ourselves and others. We no longer force our creativity. We rest when our bodies are tired. We take time to be more inwards when we are feeling sensitive. Likewise, we no longer attempt to force a situation or demand that others change, recognising that everything unfolds according to its own divine choreography. In this state of surrender, we find alignment and tranquillity with our authentic nature, allowing our creativity and lifeforce to flow freely and effortlessly.

As souls embodied in human form, it is our divine duty to look after our 'soul suits'—our bodies—just like we would take care of any other living being. We must treat our bodies with the same level of attentiveness and nurturance, listening to its needs and taking steps to maintain its wellbeing.

INVITATION

Right now, you will benefit from slowing down and taking a step back in order to gain some perspective.

When you have a strong passion for something or someone, it's natural to become fully engrossed and dedicate your time and energy to that new pursuit, relationship, or possession. While the excitement of a blazing passion is exhilarating, excessive fervour can lead to burnout, affecting both yourself and the situation at hand. It's important to strike a balance and avoid reaching a feverish state. The chances of success from this sort of intense heat are pretty slim, which is why it is better to take things at a slower pace — a nice slow burn can keep the candle lit. Moving too quickly can prevent us from seeing the bigger picture and the small warning signs that can escalate into bigger problems. Pause and reflect on what's happening around you. Ask yourself, "What's really going on here? Is there anything I have been missing?" By being more mindful and self-aware, you maintain a healthy balance and prevent being consumed by your passions, making hasty decisions, or stepping into something too soon without fully considering the consequences.

However, if things in your life are moving too slowly for you, try to sit back and enjoy the ride. Prioritise slowing down and resting. If you are feeling tired of what's happening in a situation, the message is to sleep on the issue. You will gain the clarity you need from a good night's rest. Slow down and let the rest come easy.

The Golden Key of Water

The *Golden Key of Water*, concealed in the west, holds the transformative power to unlock the innate qualities of emotional depth and adaptability within our psyche. It opens the doorway to our intuitive wisdom and guidance, helping us make wise decisions and navigate life's challenges with clarity.

Like a gentle rainfall nourishing the earth, the *Golden Key of Water* reminds us of the transformative power of love and compassion in creating harmony and balance within ourselves and the natural world. It teaches us the healing and purifying nature of tears, releasing emotional burdens and allowing for renewal and growth. Just as a river flows effortlessly, the water element shows us through its example the art of surrender, inviting us to trust in the natural currents of existence. It beckons us to dive into the depths of the unknown, to set sail to shores outside of our comfort zone.

31. Listen Closely

Your human shell is calling for your attention. Listen to your body

CARD WISDOM

The word 'heart' begins with the word 'hear'. When we listen first, we can act from that most informed and integral place within, to better fit ourselves into the universal song harmoniously. A true maestro of music doesn't merely commence playing at their own whim to take the lead within a composition. Instead, they allow themselves to be led and swayed by the music itself, ensuring they harmonise seamlessly with the ensemble of other instruments. They are guided and moved by the music to be in harmony with other instruments. Sometimes that means not playing at all, allowing the music to breathe.

In modern society, becoming comfortable with silence is not easy. We live in a world of noise and constant stimulation, having 24/7 contact with what is happening, anywhere on the planet. We unconsciously avoid silence and become anxious when there is no noise, yet silence is rich.

When we silence our mind and tune in to our breath, we enter the space of our very own peaceful void of 'no-thing' — similar to the euphoric peace we feel when submerged underwater, with only a silent hum of nothingness. Time stretches, and the space within us we create—which we usually fill with distractions—becomes comfortable.

This is the key. Don't fill yourself up with what is not meant for you, out of fear of emptiness. Lean into those empty spaces, find peace there, and listen to the silence. In this space, we come to know ourselves better, listening to what we really need in the here and now through all streams of consciousness. Here, we are detached from outside noise or mental chit-chat that obscure what really needs our attention, away from the noise that has us running from time and the real essence — *our* essence.

Listening is not a cerebral process, nor a function only of the ears — it is an open sensitivity. When we understand something, we say, "I see", which has nothing to do with our eyes. Ears are merely a channel for this earthbound sensation. What we hear we also see, smell, feel, and touch.

Listening deeply through all our senses opens our 'hearing' to the song of the earth, so we can also add to the grand orchestra of life and be in harmony with natural order.

INVITATION

Have you been ignoring the whispers of your body? Have you been spending too much time in your mind? This can conjure up bad habits. This card asks you to review your relationship with your body.

Listen deeply to what your body is yearning for right now — away from outside noise and ego-driven desires, away from what you 'think' you need now, away from what you 'think' you should do and what others expect of you. This is all preventing you from getting what you really need. Do you need to rest, or play, or stretch, or dance? What sorts of activities would best suit how your body feels today? What would be most beneficial to you? What food does your body need to feel good right now? Be mindful to distinguish between your ego-mind and your body's voice speaking.

Find a quiet and peaceful space where you can sit or lie down comfortably and take a few deep breaths to relax your body and calm your mind.

Visualise a radiant light or a beautiful colour spreading throughout your entire body, from the top of your head to the tips of your toes. Pay attention to any sensations, feelings, or areas that catch your awareness. Allow each part of your body to have a voice and speak to you. Listen attentively to what they express, with no judgement or criticism. Note any insights or messages that come up. Show appreciation for your body's wisdom and ability to communicate with you. Embrace yourself with a gentle hug and express gratitude for this connection.

When you feel ready, gently return to the present moment, carrying the insights and appreciation with you. Be gentle with yourself. Approach your body delicately each day, asking how they feel, like a friend would do.

No day is going to be the same; as your body moves in its cycles, work with your 'soul-suit', honouring times of rest, and not pushing yourself to your limit. You are not a robot. It is time to honour the voice and the callings of your human shell. They're ringing for your attention — are you going to take the call?

32. Detoxify

Watch your thoughts and what you are consuming.
Time for a mind–body–soul detox.

CARD WISDOM

When we think of 'detox', we immediately think of our diet. However, while mindful of the foods we choose for our health, we must also be consciously aware of everything else we consume. We must be mindful of what media we consume, what we listen to, what we read, who we surround ourselves with, and the conversations we have with ourselves and others.

Just as we can't expect to stay physically healthy by consuming a steady diet of processed junk food, we can't expect to maintain a healthy mind by constantly feeding it with negativity. Constant exposure to negative thoughts and emotions can have detrimental effects on our mental health. While it's okay to indulge in negative thoughts and emotions from time to time, constantly obsessing over things we can't control is not healthy for our souls. Negativity is also harmful to those around us, as it can be contagious. By constantly feeding ourselves with negativity, we're also force-feeding it to our friends and family. Therefore, it's essential to be mindful of our thoughts and emotions and strive to maintain a healthy, balanced brain. While we can't control every aspect of our lives, we can control our response to them. By choosing to focus on positive thoughts and emotions, we can cultivate a healthy and resilient mind that can navigate the ups and downs of life with grace and ease.

Falling back into unhealthy patterns is easily done and we mustn't beat ourselves up about it. Remember, we have the power to choose what nourishes our souls in every moment. We decide which thoughts to embrace and which to let go. It's within our control to curate our mental diet, discarding what no longer serves us. As much as it sometimes feels like it's out of our control, we always have options on the mental menu we choose from. We can actively decide to give our mind the balance it craves, opting for the positive options, or we can choose to feed it a steady diet of junk and wallow in the negative repercussions.

INVITATION

Examine what you are consuming and consider whether it is either nourishing or depleting your energy.

To begin the process, assess what needs to be detoxified and how. First, take a closer look at any unhealthy life habits, such as excessive phone usage, unhealthy eating patterns, or if you are surrounded by negative influences. Additionally, evaluate your coping mechanisms and identify any unhealthy patterns that are present. These factors could all be taking a toll on your overall wellbeing and are the areas that warrant a detox.

Mind detox: Limit your screen time and reduce exposure to negative media. Instead, engage in activities that are inspiring and stimulate your mind positively, such as reading soul-stirring books, listening to uplifting music or podcasts, and practising mindfulness or meditation. Allow your mind to rest and recharge by taking breaks from constant stimulation.

Body detox: Focus on nourishing your body with a balanced array of nutritious foods. Pay attention to what you consume and make choices that support your overall health. Incorporate regular exercise or physical activities that bring you joy and help release toxins from your body. Stay hydrated by drinking plenty of water and herbal teas.

Spiritual detox: Create sacred spaces or moments for introspection and connection with your inner self. This can include meditation, prayer, or spiritual practices that resonate with you. Reflect on your beliefs and values and consider how they align with your actions and choices. Surround yourself with positive energy and distance yourself from relationships that drain your spiritual vitality.

These processes are an opportunity for reflection, starting anew, and realigning yourself with what brings you joy, fulfilment, and overall wellbeing. Embrace nourishing activities that replenish your energy. Set clear boundaries to protect your energy and ensure a healthy balance.

You can create a space for positive change whilst also taking the steps to integrate your higher self. Detoxify your vessel and become a clear channel for the Divine.

33. Go with the Flow

Loosen your grip and release control and expectations of the outcome. Be open to compromise.

CARD WISDOM

Going with the flow—where there are no wrong decisions, regrets, or expectations—is an art. We can let life flow effortlessly, like watercolours on a blank canvas, guided by the intuition of our spirit. With each brushstroke, we blend light and dark shades, embracing the beautiful mess, and creating a masterpiece. It takes courage to paint on a blank canvas with no idea of where the painting is heading, with no intention of what the final piece will look like. Life isn't meant to be painted between the lines of a predetermined colouring book. A true masterpiece is made with spontaneity — risking it all, making instinctive, spontaneous decisions, and going with the flow of inspiration from moment to moment. Creating with the eyes of compromise will help, too, when things don't work out the way we once envisioned, or when we work to create with others in mind.

Living completely in flow requires not clinging to anything — whether that be an outcome, a spouse, a home, an object, a way of being, a moment in time, or even our own sense of identity. We are always in a state of perpetual change and evolution, so it's vital to remain receptive to our natural progression. Whether we encounter moments of joy or hardship, we must approach each experience with an easy-going and accepting mindset, allowing all to unfold as it's meant to. Each experience has the potential to teach us, offering us valuable lessons that contribute to our spiritual growth. By embracing this, we learn to let go of obstacles and disappointments, trusting that everything is happening for our highest good. As we observe and experience life, we must resist the urge to control or manipulate its direction, allowing it to flow like a river.

Water flows effortlessly, offering its gentle embrace. It doesn't act as a barrier or oppose us. Instead, water follows its destined path, a relentless force that cannot be stopped. It moves forward, never backward, symbolising adaptability, resilience, and fluidity. Since we are mostly composed of water, we can tap into this inherent power. When we encounter obstacles in life, rather than fighting against the current or resisting the flow, we can learn from water's wisdom. By aligning ourselves with the natural flow, like swimming in a rushing stream, we find stillness and rest. With ease and patience, we reach our intended destination, just as a small drop joins the vast sea.

INVITATION

The fluidity of water gently beckons you to surrender to its guiding current that steers you towards your dreams. Instead of resisting the universal flow, it's time to trust in its wisdom and release your grasp on rigid narratives. Do you tightly cling for dear life to grudges, regrets, or expectations, like rocks in a rushing river? Or are you resisting change, exerting excessive control, disregarding your intuition, avoiding feedback or constructive criticism, procrastinating, or being indecisive? Regardless of how this looks in your life right now, this card carries a crucial message: practise the art of letting go.

Begin by identifying any unconscious attachments and expectations that create stress, and consciously release them. Embrace the relinquishment of control, extend forgiveness to yourself and others, and acknowledge that some things lie far beyond your jurisdiction. Additionally, be willing to embrace flexibility and remain open to compromise. Allow your plans and expectations to adapt and evolve when needed. Cultivate a flexible mindset that welcomes spontaneity and embraces new possibilities.

Compromising doesn't have to be a win—lose situation. When you release resistance and open your heart to infinite possibilities, trust emerges. Whatever life presents to you, no matter how disruptive it may initially appear, it holds a deeper purpose for your soul's expansion. Instead of looking for faults, look for the potential. Opening your heart to compromise is a win—win. Remember, it is all an invitation.

Anticipate the unexpected. Dream your dreams but set them free. Let them float and sail in their own direction, without attachments to the outcome. Know that your dreams have a life of their own. As your dreams gain momentum, you may be surprised by how different they look from your original projections ... but relax. Open your heart to other possibilities. Spirit has better plans for you. Have faith!

34. Heart's Treasure Chest

Open your treasured heart and share your riches with the world. Equally, allow yourself to receive.

CARD WISDOM

Anyone reading the words 'treasure chest' would automatically envision a large wooden chest brimming with gold and jewels. Here lies the paradox to finding our treasure, our 'purpose'. People think it is 'out there' somewhere in the universe, waiting to be dug up and discovered. They spend their days searching for a hidden map that will lead them to that one 'X-marks-the-spot' destination where their gold of happiness lies. Some think that they might find their map in school, or down another career path, or with a spouse, or in another country. But the treasures we seek are within our very own chests, and the very map we seek isn't something to be 'found'. The pathway and the journey back to our hearts are where the bountiful riches lie.

As our inner quest starts to reach new heights, the treasures of the outside world lose their lustre. We stop looking outside of ourselves for our 'calling' and stop searching for everything we think we need. We realise our lives are not scripts, or plans, or mapped-out journeys. There isn't an 'X-marks-the-spot' destination for happiness. There is nowhere to go, nothing to search for, as we have already arrived. The only journey we must take is inwards. The journey back to our hearts is the destination.

When we open the treasure chest of our hearts, we find the overflowing peace that was already there. A wealth that is not dependent on external trappings and senses screaming for gratification. We hold the jewels and the purest gold of love, compassion, and strength. So much so, that the chest is overflowing. The golden love we find is what we must share with the world.

When we keep our hearts closed, they lie like buried treasure chests in the deep waters of our being, and we end up feeling lost and perhaps even becoming egocentric and greedy. But when we dig deep enough and open our hearts' treasure chests and share our love and what we love with the world, we find true happiness. This is our purpose.

INVITATION

Spirit is guiding you to share your riches—which are your love, your joy, your laughter, and your gifts—more with others. It is easy to forget that your small, positive actions, your words and deeds, and the love you share make a huge impression on the world, creating radiating, rippling effects that influence everyone. This card reminds you that your contribution doesn't need to be something over the top and flashy to create a transformative impact. Spread love to those around you, compliment strangers, or partake in small, kind gestures with no thought of gain for yourself. In sharing, you find you feel even more fulfilled.

The love you carry is limitless, so share it generously. But also, allow yourself to receive. If you give too much, you block the blessings that want to come through to you and equally, you don't allow others the chance to share their heart's treasure. Spirit sees that you are a very giving person, so you deserve to receive the love you give. Let someone do something nice for you, accept the compliment, and ask for help. This card also highlights that you have struggled with this lately. You are worthy and it's not a 'hassle' to allow people to do something nice and out of their way for you. You are precious, and others deeply acknowledge this. Allow yourself to be cherished when others offer it. Enjoy it.

A practice to help you open your treasured heart is by writing yourself a self-affirming letter. Start with, "Dear [your name]", then in writing acknowledge and appreciate the strengths, accomplishments, and qualities you admire about yourself. Reflect on your dreams, desires, and the things that bring you joy. Embrace your vulnerabilities and challenges. Write about the lessons you've learned and how you've grown, and what you hope to achieve in the future. Offer words of encouragement, love, and support to yourself. Write as if you were talking to a dear friend. End the letter with powerful statements of self-love and belief in your abilities.

Read the letter to yourself, allowing the words to resonate with your heart. Keep the letter in a safe, treasured place, to revisit whenever you need a reminder of your worth and strength.

35. Peace of Mind

**Set peace of mind as your highest priority
and organise your life around it.**

CARD WISDOM

The mind can go in a thousand directions, but when the mind is on the pathway of peace, one is fast-tracked towards touching truth.

With the improved standards of living in today's world, we suffer from overstimulation — from the news feeds on the internet, social media, and television, to the endless barrage of outside forces reaching for our attention. This modern mindset sends us on non-stop flights to overwhelm.

When we operate from a busy-minded state of awareness, we know little about pure peace. The word 'peace' is something we understand in abstract, but often not in practice. We have moments of silence, but not really feeling at peace. In most cases we have just shut up momentarily, but we are still tense and confined in the mind, like a city park shut off from activity. Deep peace is like having a 'country silence' within.

Peace and perfection are not linked. It would be nice to have everything perfectly aligned, figured out, and peaceful all the time. Life doesn't work like that. Our true selves are already peaceful, so in order to remember and create more for ourselves, we must simply be peace — we must live peace, think peace, breathe peace. We cannot seek peace from places in the world around us whilst our minds are in chaos and conflict.

Peace starts with unconditional love, acceptance of ourselves and others, and acceptance of where we are, of our place in the universe and the oneness of all things. Peace is not a place or a thing to be found that might give us the slight sensation of it. It's not just a short-lived slowing down — taking a holiday, going for a quiet walk in a park, opening a book, or switching on the TV. It is a state of mind. External stimuli only ease our minds into momentary tranquillity. True and lasting inner peace emanates from within, deeply ingrained like a still lake that beautifully mirrors the serene flight of a gentle dove. It requires our consistent and intentional engagement, akin to a dance of trust and surrender, where we allow our very cells to relax into the essence of our being. It is a profound connection to who we are and where we are, a silent celebration of this relaxation.

Peace is also a practice, just like yoga, involving showing up to self with pure presence, to mindfulness, and to deep awareness. It is practised patience, acceptance, balance and grace, a portal to higher states of reality and possibility. With time, it can become an integrated internal support system and a state of receptive consciousness.

INVITATION

If you are struggling with worries or feeling triggered, detach yourself from it all. Release your aggravations and don't allow yourself to be bothered by them. Find harmony within yourself, and do not look to the outer world to provide assurance. If something or someone has been testing your patience, now is the time to come back to love. Your highest self only takes actions accordingly when you come from a place of peace and unconditional love rather than from a triggered place of agitation, hate, and pain — from where there will be no gain.

Find your way to your own peace of mind at this very moment. Maybe it is finally ticking that important thing you've been delaying off your to-do list today, or reaching out to someone who you have been meaning to contact. You will free up lots of space in your mind, easing the heaviness weighing on your shoulders and the underlying anxiety that is quietly eating away at your subconscious.

When feeling anxious, use deep, conscious breathing as a bridge to divine peace. Deep breathing calms the nervous system, activates your relaxation response, and brings attention to the present moment. Take a slow, deep breath in through the nose, expanding the abdomen fully. Hold briefly, then exhale slowly through the mouth, releasing tension and stress. Continue this pattern, with each breath slower and more relaxed. Focus attention on the breath entering and leaving the body. Stay in this state of deep breathing and mindful awareness for a few minutes, or as long as desired.

Take the time to reconnect your mind, body, and spirit. There is no need to worry about the future; do what you can today without pressure and ask for help from others. You are loved and supported, and everything will be fine. One day, one step, and one breath at a time.

36. Reflection Time
Be honest with yourself.

CARD WISDOM

The reason we see our reflection in water is because Mother Gaia purposefully created it that way. Before mirrors, we looked into the water to see our reflections. Water is a direct connection to our emotional bodies and our feminine, yin aspects. Our ancestors knew that the reason we see our reflections in water is because it is a divine mirror for our emotional bodies. The alchemy of water teaches us about passive receptivity, purity, and flow. Sometimes calm and serene, sometimes wild and turbulent, but always flowing towards its destination.

It is not only water that is a mirror to our inner emotional state — life is a mirror, forever reflecting the unconscious parts of our psyche. As our experience of life is an experience of thought, our inward perception becomes our reality. The external world is never the problem, it's our internal perception that creates the problems. Life is just a sequence of symbols and outcomes. Good and bad moments do not exist, only the meaning we assign to them. The outside world just provides us with feedback to the congruence of our thoughts so we can grow, learning to love more.

Triggers and things that irritate us are flashing like a warning light on the parts of our internal world which are ready to be healed. Our mission is to discover what we don't love and learn to love it. The people who get on our nerves the most are amongst our greatest teachers.

By changing the inner image of ourselves, we will change the world in which we live. As Anaïs Nin reminded us, "We don't see things as they are, we see them as we are."

INVITATION

This card serves as a magic mirror, a reflection of your higher consciousness, reminding your soul of its original purity and purpose.

We can only see things within others that we see within ourselves, and we can only meet people as deeply as we've met ourselves. Be honest with yourself now. Create sacred time to partake in some mirror work, which involves having an honest pep talk directly to yourself in a mirror about what you have been denying and preventing yourself from facing. Face your shadows head-on, and then switch the discussion to give yourself compliments and words of encouragement — be your biggest fan! As important it is to look at our shadows, it is equally as important to look at our goodness, our strengths, and inner beauty. Though it can be daunting at first to face ourselves in such a raw and intimate way, this deep internal work is essential for our soul ascension. Over time, this work will turn into play, as the depth to your self-love strengthens.

You might want to explore *scrying*. This intuitive divination practice involves gazing into a reflective or translucent surface to receive guidance, insights, or information about the past, present, or future. By allowing images, symbols, or impressions to arise from your subconscious, you access deep, intuitive information. To begin, choose a scrying tool like a crystal ball or a bowl of water. Clarify your intention for your scrying session and formulate a clear question or topic in your mind. Then, relax and enter a meditative state. Gaze deeply into the scrying tool by softening your eyes (don't stare); notice any mental images, feelings, or intuitive insights that arise. Allow your attention to rest on the surface while maintaining a relaxed and open awareness. Trust your intuition and let the impressions come without judgement or analysis.

After the session, reflect on what you experienced. Consider the potential meanings behind the impressions you received. Record your insights in a journal to revisit later; but instead of writing your experience, why not try also drawing it? This could provide a different perspective and reveal patterns, symbols, or connections that may not have been apparent through written descriptions alone.

The reflective waters want to assure you that by facing any sticky situations head on, you will grow. Your willingness to be honest will lead to unlocking a shift within your reality. Have patience and be open to any, and all, possibilities. Sometimes the truth will be sad or initially worrisome, and sometimes it will be anything but what you thought it would be, but it will free you. It will always be—in some way, shape, or form—liberating!

37. Release

**Allow yourself to feel in order to heal.
Release what no longer serves you.**

CARD WISDOM

The water inside each of us connects us to all of life. It connects us to the past and the future. It has been up in the clouds and in the rain; on the snow-capped mountains, in the streams and rivers, and in the vast oceans and seas of the earth. The water that flowed across the body of Gaia millions of years ago is the same water we drink and swim in today. In our blood, we have the same water that passed through a dinosaur. Water possesses the ability to retain information. Within our bodies, it flows abundantly, and our emotions, akin to ever-changing water crystals, reflect this fluidity. We are shaped by influences, intentions, and thoughts, yet there is an immutable and intangible essence that remains constant.

Our bodies are composed of approximately 60 per cent water, and within each cell, this water carries memories. These memories hold emotions that can affect how we feel. Just like the flow of water, these emotions need to move and be released. If we try to contain them like a dam, we risk overwhelming ourselves, leading to an eventual eruption of emotions. Our emotions are just energy-in-motion, generated from within. Energy can only ever be transformed. Therefore, we must take control of our lives and become alchemists to our own lifeforce, especially when it comes to transforming our heavier emotions into more positive actionable energy.

External stimuli can only affect us if we allow them to. We must move with the flow of our emotions, joining with their fluidity but not being captured by them. Remaining unattached to fluctuations in mood or feeling, we welcome all emotions, witnessing them. At this level of awareness, we choose how we react to situations, changing how we feel in an instant. Suppressing emotion creates a dam, resulting in stagnation, energy blocks, and dis-ease in our bodies. Release is thus an important wellbeing practice.

Mother Nature expresses her emotions the same way, between her sunny moments and moody, grey moments and storms. We too must honour every mood we are in, allowing it to pass. Bottling up our emotions only later leads to destructive volcanic explosions.

INVITATION

You have been fighting the ebb and flow of your own feelings—denying your pain, hurt, anger, or sorrow—and attaching yourself to a heavy emotion and letting it drown you. When you attempt to constrict yourself from experiencing your emotions, the risk of blocking the flow may cause sporadic aggressive outbursts.

The human experience encompasses a range of emotions that we all go through. It's unrealistic to expect constant positivity and love for life. Life has its ups and downs, like the ebb and flow of waves in an ocean. Emotions are natural and should not be labelled as 'good' or 'bad'. Feeling is an essential part of being human, and it's important to honour all emotions. It's not about being 100 per cent happy all the time; we are meant to experience the full spectrum of feelings.

Cherish your emotions. Learn from them. It's when we build a relationship and an understanding with our emotions that we can relieve our inner tension. What will give you peace of mind right now? Maybe it's talking something through with a friend, or some emotional release through physical movement, including dancing, yoga, running, punching a pillow, or any exercise that moves and releases energy from your body.

One effective method is the emotional release ritual. Write down on paper your emotions and the things you wish to let go of, free from filters or judgements. Fold the paper and place it in a bottle, symbolising the containment of these emotions. Seek out a serene and peaceful outdoor space. Breathe deeply, feeling the weight of the emotions held within. When you are ready, safely burn the paper within the bottle, witnessing the flames consume what has been weighing heavy on your heart. For the final step of liberation, find a nearby body of water and release the ashes, visualising all attachments washing away. Embrace the liberating feeling of lightness that comes from letting go.

Alchemise your painful emotions through play—art, exercise, dance—and be active and creative. Release all that no longer serves you.

The soul would have no rainbow if the eyes had no tears.

—John Vance Cheney

38. Surrender

**Dance with what is rather than what isn't.
Make the most of the situation.**

CARD WISDOM

Life isn't about waiting for the storm to pass. It's about learning to dance in the rain.

—Vivian Greene

This memorable saying from the British writer is well-loved for a reason. It reminds us to not let the negativity of the world weigh us down, not allow a bad day or moment to overshadow the good days or hide the sun that shines in our soul. It's about allowing ourselves to dance and to find peace, love, and gratitude whatever the weather — internally or externally.

As humans, we have a misconception of rain. We think of it as an inconvenience that makes us feel miserable. We tense up and run at the sight of it to find shelter. We roll our eyes and curse at the sky, begging for the sunshine to come back. It's like the feeling many of us have — wanting to run away when something bad happens that we can't control. Instead of facing it, it's easier to retreat inside ourselves and turn to unhealthy coping mechanisms.

But if there was no rain there would be no flowers and no life. What if, instead of cursing, we loved the rain? What if we sang for its arrival, dancing and praising the sky for bearing down droplets of love, giving birth to more life? Sure, the rain will get us wet. Perhaps it will be cold and slightly displeasing. It might mess up our hair. But there is much more to life than unpleasantness and minor inconvenience. We must *choose* to experience joy — dance, sing in the rain, and let the water wash away the worries of the world, singing for its return, in thanks for more life and for this life!

In a similar way, we mustn't just withdraw when there's a crisis, or something seemingly troublesome is going on. It's a reminder to surrender, face it, and embrace it. Move forwards, make the most of the situation, rather than just wait for the problem to disappear. A little rain won't hurt us, just as many of the situations that fall in front of us (ones we may not like) won't hurt us either if we choose it so. They'll only strengthen us with the right attitude of gratitude.

The alchemy of rain teaches us to let things roll off our shoulders. We can't always forecast our future, so we need to adapt to change and avoid becoming so angry and irritable over the smallest of inconveniencies.

INVITATION

Gaia and your guides are fully aware of the difficulties and challenging times you are currently facing. It may seem like one thing after the other causing havoc in your life. However, take comfort in knowing that significant improvements are on the horizon, and smoother sailing seas await you. Although it may require time and effort, the key to your progress lies in your willingness to surrender. Whether you are grappling with loss, going through a breakup, dealing with health issues, or facing personal setbacks, surrendering is essential to your healing. Surrender involves acknowledging the reality of your circumstances, releasing resistance, and embracing peace and acceptance. It empowers you to navigate challenges with grace, resilience, and an open mind, leading to profound personal growth and transformation.

Although it may be challenging to comprehend at this moment, you must hold strong trust that what is happening is for your highest good and soul's evolution. The universe operates in mysterious ways, always providing what you truly need, and it is vital to trust the divine plan. Focus on making the most of your current situation, doing your part, and allowing the universe's energy to flow.

Repeat this empowering mantra, or sit with it during a meditation to strengthen your surrendering journey: *I surrender to the flow of life, and I have faith that everything works out for my highest good*.

In the midst of your surrender, engage in activities that bring joy to your heart without attempting to challenge or change the circumstances. Dance, sing, laugh, and cultivate inner peace and joy in the present moment, even when things seem gloomy. Lighten your spirit, for everything is aligning in your favour, and the reasons for this will soon become evident.

39. Unfoldment

Your inner work is paying off! Blossom into your greatness and be sure to integrate what you have learnt from any recent experiences.

CARD WISDOM

It is not abnormal for the seekers of self-discovery to feel like they lived multiple different lifetimes. Each stage of our personal growth and development can feel like a past life. Some days growth can be so immediate, we cannot even remember the person we were yesterday, or five minutes ago.

The opening of the personality to reveal the true self is much like the unfoldment of a flower — one petal opening after another ultimately to reveal the real self in the centre. As we pluck away the parts of our personality that are no longer useful, what emerges over time is a new sense of self, with a healthier, inner understanding of the unification of reality. Each layer of self that is shed turns out to have been an illusion that could just as well be labelled as 'who I am not'.

Lotus flowers are wonderful representations of divine unfoldment. Strongly rooted in the mud of a lake, their stems reach up to the surface and their petals sit peacefully. At night they sink below the surface to rest, then rise with the new light of day. Just as our own spiritual paths unfold, we too open up to the light, from darker, muddier periods of our journey.

Like the lotus flower, our souls are always reaching for the light to fulfil their karmic destiny, even in periods of darkness and times of deep rest. Our dark times amongst the sludge can seem messy and uncomfortable whilst we're stuck there, deep under it; but darkness is just as necessary as light is for our self-improvement. When in its time of darkness, a lotus effortlessly integrates its cycles, so it can continue to thrive and radiate on the surface edge. We, too, must learn to integrate the lessons we learn, in our own times of darkness. This is the groundwork. We should allow ourselves to fully absorb what we gain from our experiences, not letting the tougher times bury us to death, but instead, allowing the lessons to nourish and prepare us to make a strong breakthrough and blossom beautifully into the higher light of self.

Darkness allows the integration of nourishment received during the hours of light, but it is also vice versa; light hours absorb the sustenance gained from the dirty work of the tougher times in darkness. The universe won't give you more than you can handle.

INVITATION

The gentle currents of water carry a profound message — take one step and one day at a time and go at your own pace, there is no rush.

You do not need to force growth upon yourself or be driven by 'spiritual ambition' for your spiritual elevation. Growth is a natural process, which must be left to its own innate timing. Your spiritual development is always unfolding, even when you aren't aware of it or you're feeling stuck. Allow the place within you that naturally wants to follow the light to do so at its own pace.

Drop your ego and put an end to comparing yourself to others. It is very normal to fall into this human fallacy, but it is not in the least necessary. Comparison invites distinctions between inferiority/superiority, distracting you from your potential. Instead, focus on fulfilling *your* destiny and potential. Listen to your intuition, joy, and body to determine what feels aligned — just because something is right for someone else, doesn't mean it is for you. Because let's be frank, there is always going to be somebody who you feel is more talented, more beautiful, intelligent, better off or (supposedly) happier than you are. Equally, there will be people with less than you, too. For true happiness in your human form, you must focus on fulfilling your destiny, with what feels good for you and *only you*.

Trust in your unique path and the wisdom gained from your experiences. Integrate deeply all that you have gained from recent experiences and hardships — they strengthen your soul. Be gentle and kind with yourself as you do so. Practise self-compassion by offering understanding and forgiveness to yourself for any perceived shortcomings or mistakes, and embrace and use them as stepping-stones for growth. Express gratitude for the lessons and blessings that have come from them. You are powerful and you can share your wisdom with the world. Nurture yourself and stay aligned with your true essence, and you will continue to evolve on your spiritual path, unfurling your lotus petals one by one.

40. Voyage of the Heart

Get out of your comfort zone!
Your heart wants to sail somewhere new.

CARD WISDOM

Most people today would agree that the 1969 moon landing has been one of the greatest achievements in the history of human exploration to date. But there is another endeavour of exploration that has largely gone uncelebrated, though it is in some ways far more extraordinary. That is the first navigation of our own lands, right here on Earth. Unlike the journey to the moon, Indigenous explorers set off from their homelands without a planned route for where they were heading, or what they might find. Looking for new lands to call home, they voyaged into the vast unknown, with no means of using a compass or GPS. They navigated their journey by observing the ocean and the sky, by reading the stars and the waves. The colour of sky, the position of the sun, the shapes of clouds, and the direction from which the swells were heading, guided them by day. The rhythms of the ocean and pathways of the stars guided them by night.

In ancient times, Polynesian peoples sailed in *wa'a kaulua* canoes crafted with natural island materials, using stone tools, and only able to carry a crew of a dozen. Wayfinding in such a manner, in today's world, would seem like a hair-raising challenge — spending weeks on end on these boats that were bound by braided vegetable fibres instead of industrial metals. For the Polynesian wayfinders, it involved a deep and sacred connection to the earth and a fluency and knowledge of the planet's patterning and movements. Where the average person admires shining stars or soaring seabirds, wayfinders see constellations as their navigational guardrails, and gulls as clues for what lies ahead.

The people of the Pacific are intimately tied to the ocean. This dates back to the deep reverence their ancestors had for the sea, told through old tales and legends, which featured mighty ocean gods and goddesses. Their art, made from shells, coral and other marine materials, found its way into many Hawai'ian chants and songs. The people of Polynesia regard the vast ocean with awe and respect, deeply integrating it into their culture. It is not only essential for survival—providing food and transportation—but beyond practical significance, they believe the ocean is a living entity with its own spirit. They hold a profound respect for its power and unpredictability, viewing themselves as part of a larger ecosystem that includes the ocean. They recognise that their actions also impact the health of the ocean, as well as the life that lives within it. No other culture has embraced the open seas so fully.

INVITATION

Gaia has guided you to draw this card to encourage you to embark on a transformative journey. She is telling you it's time to trust your soul's compass and take a leap of faith into uncharted waters. The waves of water want to assure you that although you may not have all the answers or know the exact destination, you are heading in the right direction.

To start this journey, cultivate courage and let go of the fear of the unknown. Recognise your comfort zone as the real danger zone, with growth and new experiences lying beyond its boundaries. Challenge yourself to face your fears and do the thing that scares you the most. Whether it's trying something new, pursuing a passion, or adopting a different approach, embrace opportunities to explore new ways of experiencing yourself and the world.

Don't waste time hesitating in the port when exciting opportunities await. If you hesitate and miss the ship, you may miss out on a significant chance and such an opportunity may not arrive back at the harbour for a very long time. So, stop harbouring doubts — it's time to say 'yes' to taking a chance. Get onboard the ship of opportunity and count on the commands from the captain of your ship—your heart—and set sail towards new horizons.

Trust in the wisdom and support of the water element as you embark on this voyage of the heart. Embrace the challenges and the unknown, knowing that the journey holds the rewards of personal growth and self-discovery that await you on the other side. You will know you've reached your destination when you feel a deep sense of alignment, inner resonance, and fulfilment. Pay attention to signs of synchronicity, inner joy, and a profound connection with your heart's desires.

Mirror, Mirror on the World.

From the waters of her womb

her umbilical anchors all that flows forth

from her stream of consciousness.

She floods her realm;

from reds, browns, greens, and golds,

weaving together the web of life

through chlorophyll threads that create

a fertile blanket which birth her children:

leafy lifeforms, two-footed, four-footed, finned and feathered.

Creatures of the deep and sky all chasing for comfort

the cushion of her breast. We suckle her abundance.

A dance of two worlds together

both macrocosm and microcosm.

The reflection of our souls we see

in the soil and within the wisest eyes

on the wrinkling bark of an ancient elm.

Most don't speak the language of trees

but those who learn

can hear their words

in the wind that only utter,

"Do you remember?"

Remember, remember the mirror of her majesty,

the fairest one —

the All.

The Golden Key of Spirit

The *Golden Key of Spirit*, transcending all elements and realms, holds the transformative power to unlock the profound qualities of divine connection and spiritual awakening within our being. It opens the doorway to our inner wisdom and intuitive guidance, helping us to make choices aligned with our highest truth and navigate the complexities of life with clarity and purpose.

Like a sacred waterfall cascading from the heavens, the *Golden Key of Spirit* reminds us of the transformative power of love, compassion, and interconnectedness. It calls upon us to harmonise our inner and outer worlds, creating a sense of balance and unity within ourselves and the natural world.

41. Beauty

**Not everything has to be practical and dull.
Beautify every aspect of your life by adding more colour.**

CARD WISDOM

Art is the communication of the human with the sense of existence. It is the discovery of deep secrets, through penetrating the Source and the soul of All. The artist is, in this sense, a mediator between the Source and the receiver, which is then reflected to the outer world.

Art is not just an outwardly eyeful expression, everything in life is art, and art is beauty.

> *I think everything in life is art. What you do. How you dress. The way you love someone, and how you talk. Your smile and your personality. What you believe in, and all your dreams. The way you drink your tea. How you decorate*

your home. Or party. Your grocery list. The food you make. How your writing looks. And the way you feel. Life is art.

—Helena Bonham Carter

Just watch the way the steam swirls and twirls in the air, as warm tea sits in a mug on our tables — it's a symbol of warmth and comfort, an inner hug to soothe the soul, and a means to find some solace in our day. The way a smile shines upon someone's face. Taking the time to cook a meal and making it look beautiful before eating. Writing a love note and leaving it for someone to find. This is art. It's a moment in time that a photograph, a painting, or a video can easily capture, but it's so much better than any physical piece of art. It's our own symbolic moment of beauty.

Receiving a cheerful smile from a stranger or someone we love can literally make or break a day. It's the transfer of kindness and hope among humans, a silent exchange that speaks louder than words. Just like physical art itself, we embrace it because it makes us feel a certain way. The same concept that applies to smiling applies to other actions in our lives.

Every moment we are creating beauty. We are all artists, painting our lives upon the canvas of our own reality. Our perception of the world and how we choose to paint it is entirely within our control. Every sunrise presents a fresh opportunity to pick up the paintbrush that lives within our hearts and decorate our day with whatever colours and tones we wish. We can opt for a palette of passion, compassion, love, and unity, or we can choose to paint with fear and negativity. Our external experiences reflect our internal states of being. If we view the world through the eyes of fear, we will inevitably create a reality with the undertones of anxiety. However, if we view the world through a lens of love, we will paint a masterpiece that is filled with healing and happiness. We came here to create our reality, not to just face it.

INVITATION

This card signifies that you have been rushing and getting caught up in the hustle and bustle of life. As a result, you've missed out on the simple pleasures that surround you in the present moment. Gaia invites you to slow down and dedicate time to beautifying with positive intention all areas of your existence. Start by being mindful of the way you speak about yourself and others. Choose to use kind and uplifting words that give you a sense of empowerment and add value to your interactions. You can also enhance your daily routine by adding small, but meaningful, touches such as preparing your meals with care and creativity, lighting candles for yourself, displaying fresh flowers and plants, writing in a journal that feels good to touch, lavishing yourself in delicious smelling oils, savouring each sip of your coffee, or sending a hand-written letter to a loved one. Although it may be challenging to break through the practicality and rush of daily life, see beauty as an essential part of all situations you find yourself in. You have the power to mould moments into whatever shape or form you want. This practice becomes most challenging when things become ugly. Can you act in a way to bring peace and sincerity to the difficult encounter? When everyone else perceives only darkness, can you paint over it with more colour to make things brighter?

The artist's way is a path you travel and a daily practice, where you choose to pave your own way, created by the blueprint of beauty. To truly enjoy life, it's important to approach everything with love and bring beauty to every situation, rather than being too practical and goal oriented. Life is a series of singular moments woven into one, enjoyed individually as they braid together. Take time to appreciate the small things — stop to smell the flowers or look up at the stars; take long deep breaths and fully inhale all the beauty that surrounds you. An artist doesn't create art to sell a finished product; they create because they love the process of creating beauty. Approach your life in the same manner.

42. Web of Life

**Widen your social web to meet more
like-minded and fulfilling connections.**

CARD WISDOM

In the Ojibwe language, the word for 'dreamcatcher', *asabikeshiinh*, translates to mean 'spider'. A renowned story from Ojibwe mythology tells of the mysterious Spider Woman who acts as a spiritual protector for their tribe, especially protecting their land, their young children, and their newborn babies. She brought ancient wisdom and communication to the people and created, then wove, all the stars in the sky. She made soft webs to support those who were troubled to rest upon. Since she could not go to every single child at night and protect them from evil influences, she received help from the Ojibwe mothers and grandmothers, who wove webs over willow hoops, hanging them above each child's bed, to trap bad dreams and nightmares.

The circular frame of a dreamcatcher symbolises Mother Earth and everything that sustains life within her world womb. Its circular shape also represents the continuous flow of life, as there is no beginning or end to the circle of life. Dreamcatchers are also woven to look like a balanced and harmonious spider's web in a way. A bead embedded in the centre of it represents the spider. Spiritually, spiders are a symbol of the great power we all hold, the power to weave our own destiny. This is why spiders are often associated with karma and reincarnation. Web-weaving is also a metaphor for creativity — spinning our own destinies and creating our own realities. Weaving our dreams into the fabric of life, using threads of intention with the help of spirit to spin it into form. Spirals on a spider's back resemble the coiled shape of the *kundalini*, representing awakening and a sense of balance.

Spider webs are the ultimate symbol of connection, showcasing the intricate threads that bind all of life together. We are all connected through others, all woven into one. We each have a significant purpose in it all, a single thread in a web of many. The World Wide Web we have today, spun into the ether, allows us to connect from anywhere in the world, to anyone in the world ... just like magic!

INVITATION

The spirit element guides you to widen your web by weaving new, more fulfilling and loving connections into your life. Find or spend more time with your soul family, those who love you, accept you, see you, inspire you, and are inspired by you, and support your desire to grow. As you accelerate on your spiritual path, combine your energy with the like-hearted souls who share your vision for an abundant, happy life full of magic and possibility, and encourage you to live out your greatest potential.

Expand your interests and your experiences to meet with more like minds and hearts and make fresh memories with new people. Start by investigating the many ways you can put yourself out there in your community, and network to connect with other kindred spirits. As you do so, the potential for joy will increase in your life, as well as budding new, yet significant, partnerships — whether they be romance, business, or friendship.

You are so loved now, but there is so much more love to be felt, especially when you consciously put yourself out there to meet with your soul family — those who have similar interests and views on life to your own. You will also start to build a bigger—and, more importantly, meaningful—support network around you. There is a whole world out there, ready and wanting to love you.

If you haven't found your people yet, this is a sign that they are close by.

43. Ask for Help

**You can do anything, but you can't do everything.
Seek assistance to help you expand.**

CARD WISDOM

When people say, "We are all one," it isn't just a New-Age metaphor pandering for peace, love, and understanding; it is a fact. Our true selves—our conscious awareness and the deep roots of our beings—all stem from the same seed of creation. We may appear to be different, but we are not separate. Humans have an inherent connection with everything and everyone, not just on Earth, but also beyond it. The ancient phrase 'as above, so below', said to be engraved on the legendary Emerald Tablet of the *Corpus Hermetica*, describes the oneness of all that is. It reminds us that life on Earth is intricately linked to the visible stars in the sky above us, and that the microcosm and macrocosm are intensely interdependent. The human world reflects in parallel to the larger universal field.

Asking for help is not a sign of weakness, but an acknowledgment of our interconnectedness. We are not meant to navigate this journey alone. Just as we are connected to the universe, we are also connected to one another. The symbol from Hermes Trismegistus—two interconnected triangles pointing away from one another—reminds us we are part of a never-ending phenomenon. Our soul's journey extends beyond our individual selves, traversing from below to above, and ultimately becoming an integrated, inseparable part of the universe.

Our human shell has three main parts: mind, body, and spirit. Our minds are unique and separate from one another; our bodies can connect but are separated by physical space; the spirit allows us to connect directly with all other beings. The key to reaching the rest of existence is by attaining a deep connection to our own soul, which then further connects us to the world soul, the *anima mundi*.

A heart-warming story exemplifying this is the remarkable rescue of a seven-year-old girl named Amber Owen by Ning Nong, the compassionate elephant. Amber found herself in a life-threatening riptide whilst swimming in the sea on vacation in Thailand. Sensing her distress, Ning Nong rushed to her aid, extending her gentle trunk to lift Amber and keep her afloat amidst the fierce currents until help arrived. This is a powerful reminder that love and compassion transcend boundaries, bridging the perceived divide between humans and the rest of creation, uniting us in a shared experience of interconnectedness.

INVITATION

This card addresses the challenge of feeling isolated and overwhelmed while attempting to navigate life's challenges alone. Spirit compassionately acknowledges the weight that rests upon your weary shoulders, the burden of shouldering everything without respite, and the toll it takes on your emotional wellbeing.

In this moment, the gentle whispers of spirit come forth, offering solace and guidance. It is a gentle reminder you need not carry the weight of the world upon your shoulders. Asking for help is not a sign of weakness; rather, it is a testament to your strength and wisdom. It takes courage to recognise when the path becomes dark and to extend your hand in search of support.

Turn your gaze to the embrace of nature's nurturing presence, drawing upon its timeless wisdom and healing energy. Seek solace in the warm embrace of those who walk alongside you, for they yearn to lend their strength and offer help. But do not overlook the unseen forces that lovingly guide and protect you. They stand ready, waiting for your call, eager to lend their support and illuminate the path ahead. Turn inwards and ask for Great Spirit's guidance.

As you step forward and humbly ask for help, you not only empower yourself with renewed strength but also create an extraordinary opportunity for others to contribute to the greater good of all. The universal Law of Oneness teaches us we are all interconnected, and our helpful actions and kind thoughts impact the collective consciousness.

Embrace the profound truth that you are never alone. Reach out, dear seeker, and let the harmonious symphony of interconnectedness guide you towards a brighter horizon. For in seeking help, you not only find the support you crave but also give others a gift of purpose and meaning. Together, united in your shared humanity, you can illuminate the path, forging a collective journey of growth, healing, and transformation.

44. Altar of Heart

You are the altar. Adorn yourself in jewels and prayers and take part in self-care practices.

CARD WISDOM

An altar serves as a sacred space of worship, created with a specific intention — a quiet place to pray, reflect, ground the body, receive guidance, re-centre the heart, and restore the mind. It is where we reconnect with our souls, our higher selves, and the Divine. However, we do not need to be someplace outside of ourselves, like a holy place or ancient temple, in order to connect us to ourselves and our source. Our vessels are the church, our blood is the holy water, our heartbeats are the musical symphony, and our souls are the lit candle flame in the centre of our shrines.

We are the holy place. We are the altar. And much like an altar, we decorate ourselves with what is personal to us. We bless and cleanse the space and adorn it with healing gems, fabrics, and items which hold their own significance. This can also be said for how we dress and take care of ourselves, too. With intention, we become a walking sacrament.

By intentionally becoming a walking altar, we cease to search outside of ourselves for the deep connection and the peaceful place we externally seek. Whenever we feel unaligned and we need to disengage, we can simply come back to ourselves and to our breath.

The simple act of returning to our breath becomes a sacred practice, anchoring us in the present moment and reconnecting us to the divine essence within. Our breath becomes the incense that purifies our inner sanctuary, restoring balance and harmony.

INVITATION

If you have been feeling unaligned and disconnected from yourself and life around you, renew your connection by adoring and adorning the altar of your inner queendom/kingdom.

Dive into the realms of scent, touch, taste, and feeling, and give yourself the gift of self-expression. Play with colours in your clothing, dressing up in a manner that lifts your spirit, expresses your soul, and makes you feel confident, sacred, and sensual, solely for your own pleasure.

Enhance your adornment by embracing healing gems, jewels, essences, and flowers. Allow their energy and beauty to envelop you, creating a harmonious resonance within. Layer yourself in loving crystal jewellery and explore the realm of flower essences to enliven your senses.

Speak words of prayer and affirmation to your body. Stand before the mirror and embrace self-love as you acknowledge the holiness of your being.

To maintain energetic clarity, cleanse your vessel through various practices. Engage in the burning of ethically sourced incenses or herbs such as sage to purify your energy and space. Embrace the power of sound through practices like sound healing, allowing vibrations to harmonise with your cells and cleanse the waters of your inner being. Reiki and meditation can also help clear and balance your energetic field.

Engage in embodied practices such as breathwork or yoga to unify your body and spirit, promoting a state of wellbeing. Carefully choose nourishing foods and engage in self-care rituals that replenish and rejuvenate your body.

Remember, you are a walking altar, and your body is holy grounds for the Great Spirit. Do not let your shrine (your body) lose its shine. Take care of your temple. Treat it with loving respect and honour its sacredness. Prioritise self-care and self-love, for you radiate energy and vitality when you are rejuvenated — you perform better in your work, your focus and attention become clearer, and you show up fully for others and life, with an abundance of love and gifts to give.

45. Ritual

Break free from an outdated cycle.
Change your daily routine to make life more meaningful.

CARD WISDOM

Ritual vs routine — same sense but different essence, just a fine line differentiating between the two. Routine is meaningless, outcome-oriented, automatic, eyes and heart closed. Ritual is meaningful with intention, purpose, and pure presence. Both are actioned habits; what sets them apart are not the actions themselves, but the attitudes behind the actions.

Routines are actions that just need to be done, such as making our beds, taking a shower, brushing our teeth, getting dressed, and going to work. They are not seen as meaningful parts of our day — they are viewed as chores. Rituals, on the other hand, are viewed as meaningful practices.

They bring with them a real sense of intention, woven with a meditative motive. They do not have to be religious or spiritual, what matters is our subjective experience. Rituals are internally motivated by presence and engagement with the whole experience of the task. The magical power of ritual marries the mundane with the sacred. Everyday routines can become ritualistic through the power of intent.

Devotional life is enriched by repetition and routine, when carried out in a way that serves the soul, such as the use of prayer beads in many religions:

> *Counting prayers while fingering beads is a universal use. The idea behind this lies in the nature of repetition that soothes like a lullaby. It is calming and introspective.*
>
> —Manuela Dunn Mascetti

Mixing mindfulness and gratitude into our daily routine is how we shift the mundane to become a meditation — how a routine becomes a ritual. Taking a shower, for example, can become an opportunity to become mindful of our bodies and their connection to our minds, by focusing on the sensation of the water on our skin, whilst washing away any negativity from our energy bodies. Mindful eating can help food taste better, making us feel more satisfied. Even cleaning the house can be a way to become more aware of our space. Gratitude reminds us how lucky we are to live in a home and be blessed with this abundance. This allows us to sink into the present moment. Instead of feeling that chores are something that 'just need to be done', they become activities that serve positive functions in our lives, things we may even enjoy doing and look forward to. Ultimately, the more meaning we can add to our daily activities, the more motivated we become to want to do them.

By stepping back to see the bigger picture behind our daily activities, we can improve our lives as a whole, adding more richness and meaning, and helping us to view our activities as a celebration of life. Life is but one big ceremony!

INVITATION

You are being asked to look at the areas of your life that feel stagnant and outdated. It may be an unhealthy daily routine that you've undertaken, one that has run its course, no longer serving you or feeling good to you. Change your routine or put in place a new routine that serves to nourish your soul. Perhaps it is time to implement a practice like yoga, meditation, or breathwork before you rush off for a busy day's work. It is essential for your wellbeing and spiritual growth that you are dedicated to yourself, your soul, and your source. Allocate sacred time to sit with yourself and your questions.

This may be a message that one of your daily rituals is becoming a dull habit and is losing its sacredness. What can you do to breathe life back into your practice? The solution might be simple, like lighting some candles or setting an intention prior. You may even have to go lengths and put this practice on pause for a while, to reawaken its divinity and your love for it. Distance from the things we love does indeed make the heart grow fonder.

Be more mindful with your actions throughout the day. Are you running on autopilot and missing the deliciousness and pleasures of each passing moment? Add more intention behind each task. Arrive in pure presence with what you are doing. Feel each moment delicately — clean the dishes with gratitude for the fresh water and for eating a nourishing meal; eat mindfully at a slower pace; light a candle for this moment; slow down and be gentle. Can you even make filing your taxes a sacred act?

Enjoy each moment as best you can. These mundane tasks are part of living in this world, so why not make them pleasurable? Each moment is sacred, so allow yourself to feel them with more love. Life is but one big celebration. Open your heart and let it be felt.

46. Find Balance

Pull yourself out of your procrastination and better balance your time between work, play, spirituality, exercise, and relationships.

CARD WISDOM

Gaia maintains a rhythm of cycles to help her keep balance and harmony and sustain life forms to thrive. The fluctuations of temperatures over her long history is evidence of this. She creates life from antagonism — the five elements, which are the basis of her being, are all complementary and opposing forces. For example, water constrains fire, and fire commands air. Earth can either be contained by all of them or be the destroyer of them all; it is also in polarity to spirit. All these disparate forces work equally together to maintain her balance. Much the same as Gaia, we too are constantly being pushed away from our balance points — our bodies work tirelessly, yet effortlessly, to maintain homeostasis. We don't even have to think about it — our bodies were designed by the same natural wisdom that governs our universe, always striving to restore equilibrium.

Our world comprises polarities: positive and negative charges in atoms, dark and light, warm and cool, feminine and masculine. They exist throughout the natural world. The only thing untouched by nature's hand and not always in equilibrium is the domain of our mind. It is here that we bear the responsibility to take control. It is within our consciousness that the true power of balance resides. Mother Earth can teach us how to balance our opposing forces, both within ourselves and in our world.

Our mother Gaia is always serving as a guiding spirit by mirroring us through nature and the external world. She shows us that all polarities—like sun and storm, and the positive and negative energies inside us—are equally important. Allow them to coexist within and allow them to be expressed. Notice how these two energies inter-relate, and honour the expression of both in our lives. As we master the art of balancing our polar expressions, much of the suffering within life will naturally dissolve.

INVITATION

Review how you may be out of balance with your time and energy regarding the externals and internals in your life. How can you become more centred? Maybe you have been working too much, or overly obsessed with something, perhaps a relationship or money. By tuning into your inner cycles and becoming more aware of your priorities, you can take steps to restore balance and feel more centred.

One way to achieve greater balance is by changing how you allocate your time. Consider scheduling specific blocks of time for different areas of your life, such as work, play, spirituality, exercise, and relationships. This can help you create a more structured and intentional approach to your day-to-day activities. It can also help you identify areas where you may spend too much time or neglect your needs. By achieving a better balance between the various aspects of your life, you can return to a state of harmony and feel more fulfilled and content.

If you are putting off something important, weigh up your options, but don't fall victim to procrastination. Sometimes it can be very difficult to make a choice when we have multiple options that appeal to us, or if we dislike any of the possibilities. If you are unsure which direction to go, or which path to take, look within and ask yourself, "What do I need to do to move forward? Which decision would make me feel more centred and balanced?" Trusting your intuition, align yourself with the path that feels most promising. Additionally, consider asking, "What would my higher self do in this situation?" This perspective can help you envision the best possible outcome for the future you.

Pull yourself out of any procrastination, your older and wiser self will thank you for it.

47. Intuition

But what does your intuition say? To know what to do next, trust and listen to the signals sent through your human vessel from higher guidance.

CARD WISDOM

Just as birds migrate or can sense when a tsunami might hit, squirrels know when it is time to gather food for the winter, or how baby turtles know to return to the sea, we humans too have an innate intuitive sense. This intrinsic intuition is an integral part of our being, present even before our conception, as the sperm swims to meet the egg.

In days gone by, our ancestors possessed a profound connection to their intuition and inner knowing. They lived in harmony with the natural rhythms of the earth, attuned to the subtle whispers of the world around them. Unburdened by the reliance on clocks and barometers, they effortlessly knew the time and weather, sensing the shifts in nature's patterns. Their intuition, like a faithful compass, guided them through the uncertainties of life, offering insights that surpassed the limitations of the rational mind.

In our fast-paced modern existence, we have become disconnected from these innate abilities. We rely heavily on external devices and information to navigate our daily lives. Clocks control our schedules, and weather forecasts dictate our plans. Amidst the cacophony of noise, we have forgotten how to attune ourselves to the voice of our intuition and trust the wellspring of wisdom that resides within.

Yet, the wisdom of our ancestors is encoded in our DNA and patiently waits for us to awaken and embrace its guidance. As we detach from the distractions of modern life, the natural world beckons us, ready to reveal its secrets and speak to us in its own language. By rekindling our connection to our bodies and senses, we can hear Gaia's song and reclaim the gifts of our intuitive heritage, restoring the delicate balance between our inner knowing and external life. It is in this reconnection that we discover the profound interconnectedness between ourselves and the natural world.

We need to cultivate this very delicate balance — keeping our minds on and tuning into our intuition at the same time. Through meditation, we can move beyond illusion to truth. Meditation is a portal, opening ourselves to our intuition. Prayer is how we speak to God, but it is through meditation and opening our intuition that we hear the universe speak back.

Here's an intriguing possibility worth meditating on — if the possibility of our existence in alternate realities is true, it begs the question: are our future selves communicating with us and sending guidance back to us through the means of our intuition?

INVITATION

Great Spirit has guided you to pull this card as a gentle reminder to listen the wisdom of your inner whispers, and trust in the power of your intuition. In a world bustling with distractions, it's easy to overlook the subtle signs and red flags that signal misalignment. The desire to see the best in others can sometimes cloud your judgement, causing you to ignore the tightening in your chest, the intuitive warnings, and the uneasy, off-ish energy around certain individuals. However, your intuition holds the key to your wellbeing and highest alignment.

Envision your intuition as a benevolent spirit guide, a beloved friend, who is always by your side offering unwavering support and guidance. Just as a cherished human friend imparts invaluable advice through a heartfelt conversation, your intuition communicates with you through subtle language. It speaks to you through intuitive nudges, gut feelings, and a deep sense of resonance. To ignore its call is to disregard the wisdom of a trusted friend, who only wishes the best for you.

However, we don't have answering machines for our intuition to leave its message — the call will just keep on ringing until you answer. When you listen to your intuition, you honour the sacred bond between your inner self and the Divine. You recognise that this intuitive connection holds the answers you seek, illuminating the path ahead. Trusting it is an act of self-love and self-respect. Embrace the calling of your intuition with openness and receptivity. Seek solace in nature for stillness and contemplation, and pay attention to the signs, synchronicities, and subtle whispers that guide your steps. By nurturing this relationship with your intuition, you deepen your connection to your authentic self and the vast wisdom of the universe. Your intuition may just be sending you a warning sign right now. Trust it.

48. Law of Attraction

Attune your energy to higher frequencies, open your palms and your heart to the universe. Don't chase, attract!

CARD WISDOM

When we unclench our fists and minds, relinquishing our hold on the past or the future, a beautiful transformation takes place in which we open ourselves to receive in the present. This profound shift aligns with the teachings of *aparigraha*, a concept within yoga found in the ancient texts called the *Yoga Sūtras*, which encapsulates the wisdom of non-grasping and open-handedness. It is the art of staying open to receive and embracing the present moment with open arms and a receptive heart. It teaches us to remain untethered from our current possessions or circumstances and cultivate the practice of letting go. *Aparigraha* is a constant practice that frees us to stay divinely connected, receiving reality in the here and now. It allows us to connect without filtering experiences through our past traumas, future wishes, un-serving attachments, and the other ties taking our presence of mind.

When our minds are closed off—having limiting thoughts or tunnel vision—we only see what isn't possible for us. But when we align the teachings of *aparigraha* with the Law of Attraction, we understand that our thoughts and emotions play a vital role in attracting what we desire. Just as *aparigraha* encourages us to let go of attachment to outcomes, the Law of Attraction teaches us to focus on our desires with clarity and intention while detaching from the 'how' and 'when' they will manifest. By combining these teachings, we recognise that our thoughts and emotions carry a vibrational frequency that interacts with the energetic field of the universe. When we practise non-grasping and release attachment, we create a state of openness and receptivity. In this state, our desires can flow to us effortlessly, guided by the universal forces that are always working in our favour.

Both *aparigraha* and the Law of Attraction remind us of the co-creative powers we hold with the universe. Everything is energy, and cosmic forces are always working for us. That which we seek seeks us too, magnetised by the same vibration. Know that when our thoughts align with our highest visions, the universe will magnetise it to us. Our thoughts and actions attract more of the same.

When we live with open palms, not clinging to life's circumstances, incredible things come to pass.

INVITATION

Do not try to chase what you want now, you may just chase it away — even if it seems within your grasp. Now is the time to attract. Understand how the Law of Attraction operates in harmony with your focused inner work. You will naturally attract what you are calling in when you prioritise your personal growth and self-development. In doing so, you create a field that draws in the experiences and manifestations you desire. You will be drawn to what resonates with your intentions, making it crucial to embody the qualities and energy of the things you want to manifest. Recognise that you possess the power to either repel or magnify what comes your way. Try this simple embodiment exercise:

Find a serene and comfortable space. Visualise the people, things, and experiences you want to welcome into your life. See them vividly in your mind's eye, surrounding you with their presence. In every cell of your body, feel the joy, fulfilment, and gratitude that arise from having them in your. Allow yourself to fully immerse in the emotions and sensations associated with these manifestations. Breathe deeply, anchoring this vibrant energy within you. Stay in this embodied state for a few moments, savouring the experience. When you are ready, take a few deep breaths and carry this sense with you throughout your day.

By regularly practising this exercise, you deepen your connection with the people, things, and experiences you want to manifest. As you align your thoughts, emotions, and physical sensations with these, you become a magnet for their realisation. Trust that the things you want will come at the right time. The underlying fears that bring about 'chasing' behaviour, are the very same ones that result in lack and disappointment. So be patient and take a step back from actively seeking what you want. Practise embodiment and prioritise your inner work. Open your heart—and your palms—to receive from the universe that which is already on its way to you. Hold faith that the wait will be worth it, and it will come to you, exactly when you are ready.

49. Divine Love

Refocus your attention on the overflowing power of love you hold within, to help you reconnect to your divine and eternal spirit. This will aid in attracting or healing a relationship.

CARD WISDOM

The hamster wheel of personal development has the potential to become a looping obsession, one that keeps us running after the prize of deep fulfilment, shining and dangling before our eyes from a single thread of hope, always just out of reach. Instead, we should find a way to naturally embody genuine self-love. It is only by jumping out of the cage of control and criticism that we begin to truly see how far we have travelled from the joy inherent in our very being.

We must stop the chase, 'the becoming' that is fuelled by judgement, by which we feel we must earn the worthiness of love and being liked by others. We are not broken machines that need fixing to become complete or worthy of love. Love is not something we do, it is what we already are.

We change our world and the world around us when we open the silent eye of acceptance, embracing change within ourselves and those around us without grasping, as exemplified by this:

> *Love is neither dim nor blind, but rather is so far-seeing that it can glimpse around corners, around bends and even straight through walls and illusions. Instead of overlooking faults, love sees right through them, to the secrets inside.*
>
> —Vera Nazarian

The beginning of authentic love is to let those we love be themselves, and not mould them into an image of how we want them to be. Otherwise, we only love the reflection of ourselves that we see in them. Our love's true power is reflected in the space we create by allowing others to live their truth even when it differs completely from ours, without diminishing our compassion for them. Everything is ultimately love — by understanding this as *truth*, we can witness the love in all. All actions from others towards us come from a place of either a lot of love, a lack of love, or a reaching out for love. There is nothing else. Having this awareness helps to get ourselves out of victimhood, and instead, into a peaceful place of loving understanding.

INVITATION

This card is concerned with relationships: the relationships you have with lovers, friends, family, and all of creation — but ultimately the relationship you have with yourself. Refocus your attention on the overflowing power of love you hold within. This will help you reconnect to your divine and eternal spirit, then enable you to further your connections to yourself and to those around you.

Your shadows, and those of others, are standing in your light and shading your view of divine Life itself. Take off the shades that are keeping you in a dark place, so as to see clearly in full colour through the eyes of the spirit. Can you witness the perfection in yourself and those around you, just as we all are? If only you could see yourself, as those in spirit see you, you would know how loved and adored you truly are.

To call in love, turn your focus inwards and reconnect with your soul's essence. Embody the version of yourself you aspire to be in a loving relationship. Remember that the love you attract is linked to how much you love yourself. Whether in a partnership or not, remember that you are always in a relationship with yourself. The love you cultivate for yourself will shape the quality of love you can embrace from life.

If someone you love is causing you pain, witness it as a projection of their wounds, reaching out for the love they lack. See the love that's hidden beneath. Don't absorb their pain, just observe, and come back to your own internal peaceful centre; retreat from them to let things cool if need be. You cannot change a person, but you can guide them to their self-love by holding this frequency for yourself. Simply observe, allow, and centre yourself into an all-encompassing, loving awareness.

Open your heart more and more, each day. More aligned love is flowing, wounds are healing, and more hearts are opening around you. Open the gates to your heart. It is time to let more people and partnerships in. You are ready. Don't be afraid.

50. Wish Upon a Star

This is a magical moment. Make a wish and expect the very best.

CARD WISDOM

We make wishes when blowing the candle on a birthday cake, throwing coins into a wishing well, blowing the seeds of a dandelion, or seeing a shooting star. The traditions of making wishes have endured for generations, but in today's times they have turned into superficial gestures. When we delve into the roots of these rituals, we uncover the true meaning and real magic behind the mystery — an understanding grasped by seers that transcends what is perceived by vision alone.

Blowing out the candles on a birthday cake traces its origin back to ancient Greece, when people would honour Artemis, the goddess of the moon, by using a round cake with candles as an offering to her. They believed that the smoke carried up towards the heavens to reach her.

The wishing well comes from ancient Celtic traditions appeasing the Celtic goddess, Coventina. Other than being reassuring words from Jiminy Cricket, the phrase, "When you wish upon a star, your dreams come true," reflects a worldwide tradition of making a wish upon seeing a shooting star. This traces back to the second century Greek astronomer, Ptolemy, who interpreted these celestial marvels as the twinkling, watchful eyes of the gods. It was believed the veil between worlds had become exceptionally thin, allowing the stars to slip through spaces in the heavens. Shooting stars were seen as signs the Gods were peering down at Earth and therefore it was a good time to ask for what we wish for the most.

Our world comprises 'known knowns', and some are open to the possibility of the 'unknown knowns'. Beyond these hide 'unknown unknowns' which are incomprehensible celestial forces that can affect our lives. Nowadays, most people quick to dismiss that which lies hidden in unseen domains.

The surface-level action of making a wish holds deeper meanings. The sincere idea of wishes rests on the belief that divine intervention governs the life cycle of humans. In a literal sense, we can never know what runs in a deity's mind, but these ancient rituals condition a belief that higher powers can and will assist in our human and earthly concerns.

INVITATION

Look up to the stars in the sky tonight and make a wish. The gateway to Heaven through the stars has been opened, and your prayers are next in line to be answered. Trust that your wish will come true, even if it manifests in a different or better way than you initially expected. Your trust is the magic that fuels wishes, and the more trust you have the better. However, if you have fears about your future that make you feel hopeless, these fears may come true. Therefore, clear any spiritual obstacles and prepare to receive. As you make your wish to the starry sky above, imagine your words floating up in a bubble of light, passing the stars and arriving at Heaven's gate.

To make the most of this card's energy, be crystal clear on your intentions and view your life from a higher perspective. Take time for self-reflection and journalling, contemplating the broader picture of your life in this very moment. Consider your values, passions, and purpose. How do your intentions align with your higher self? How do they contribute to your personal growth and the wellbeing of others? Practise kindness and uplift others' spirits by offering a helping hand or lending a listening ear — even the smallest acts have a significant impact. You have the power to uplift and heal humanity and the earth with your presence.

Become a role model for others by embodying the values and behaviours you wish to see in the world. Live your life with integrity, kindness, and compassion, knowing that your actions can inspire and motivate others to follow suit. Fill the bucket of your breath with the blessings that reside within your inner wellspring, and contribute to the universal pool by re-filling the world's wishing well with your love!

Spread love, hope, positivity, and kindness by sending your wishes out into the universe and taking action to help others. Create hope for humanity with your prayers for peace, replenishing the waters of the collective good. With more wishes for peace and unity, the collective will shift into a higher vibration of love, and earthly blessings will pour out. Share the abundance of love and positivity that surrounds you, and be the light you wish to see in the world. Let your light shine bright and inspire others to do the same.

Remember to use your wish wisely and trust that the universe has your back.

About the Author

Introducing **Vanessa Tait**: a visionary healer, author, and eco-warrior. Armed with a background in psychology, counselling, and a range of holistic practices, Vanessa's transformative expertise takes healing to a whole new dimension. She's not just a holistic life coach, but also a certified yoga teacher, Reiki practitioner, and massage therapist. Her abilities as a healer empower individuals to unlock balance and wellbeing in every aspect of their lives.

But that's not all. Vanessa is an accomplished author and poet, channelling nature's wisdom and ancient knowledge into her powerful work. Her deep connection to sacred ecology and Indigenous ways of living in union with the land reflect her commitment to healing Mother Earth. Published in prestigious magazines and serving as editor for *Witches Magazine*, Vanessa's influence is far-reaching.

With her warm and compassionate approach, Vanessa empowers others to embark on profound journeys of growth and self-discovery. Whether through coaching, counselling, yoga, massage, or writing, she passionately encourages others to come back home to their hearts and lead fulfilling lives.

Ready to experience Vanessa's magic? Visit her website: *www.vanessatait.com* or find her on Instagram: *@themeditative_mermaid*. Embrace transformation like never before!

About the Artist

Meet **Hannah Adamaszek**: an artistic alchemist of mindfulness and serenity. Her mesmerising artworks transport viewers to a realm of tranquillity, leaving negativity in the dust. Nature's dance with the human spirit captivates her, becoming the soulful muse for her creations. Unveiling the hidden beauty within, Hannah's empowering portraits celebrate the strength of women.

But her art is more than just paint on canvas – it's a portal to reconnect with ourselves, nature, and the world. Through her passion for outdoor sports and yoga, Hannah infuses positivity and balance into her life, sharing that gift with her audience.

Hannah's talent knows no bounds; her work graces galleries worldwide, and she's been a star at events like the *OM Yoga Show*. Whether painting murals for shops, designing for fashion brands like *Chasing Rivers* and *Boho Beautiful*, or garnering attention from top blogs and magazines, including *Free People* and *The Independent*, her impact is undeniable.

Bless your eyes with more of Hannah's work by visiting her website *www.hannahadamaszek.com* or find her on Instagram *@hannahadamaszek*.

`More from Blue Angel Publishing`

Maidens of the Wheel Oracle Cards
Inner Journeys through the Cycles of the Year

Tammy Wampler

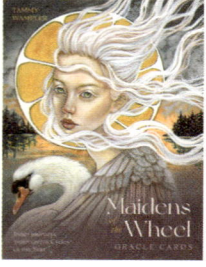

The Maidens of the Wheel have been known in many places and by many names throughout history. They dance through the cosmos, embodying inspiration and whispering guidance. They are here to empower and align you with sacred rhythms and lost traditions. Work with these elemental beings to discover harmony within the cycles of your life and embrace your true, unshakable center.

45 cards + 120-page full-colour guidebook packaged in a hardcover box.
ISBN: 978-1-922573-90-2

More from Blue Angel Publishing®

Medicine Heart Oracle

Shamanic Wisdom of the Divine Feminine

Alana Fairchild
Artwork by Sophie Wilkins

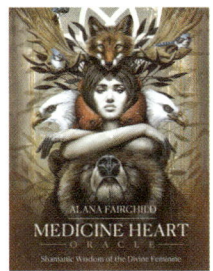

Connect with the eternal essence of Mother Earth to honour the natural wisdom and loving intelligence of your Medicine Heart. Within the soul-nurturing space of this sacred oracle, you will discover precious offerings nestled in seen and unseen dimensions. Breathe into your questioning and allow shamanic treasures from around the globe to reveal ancient pathways, creative visions and potent spirituality. You are ready to vitalise your transformational purpose, so move with the healing rhythms of Earth and Sky and enrich your life for the benefit of all.

44 cards + 368-page full-colour guidebook packaged in a hardcover box.
ISBN: 978-1-922573-80-3

More from Blue Angel Publishing®

Soul Mirror Oracle

Healing Through Divine Reflection

Sunshine Connelly

Artwork by Ana Novaes

Self-reflection is an active, ongoing, revealing and illuminating process. Within its light, you are freed into the understanding that we are all divine, all creators, all connected. Gaze into this oracle to transform fear, amplify love and welcome potent, tangible change for yourself and all the intertwining threads and consciousness of your world. Know and see yourself through the mirror of your soul — your evolving destiny awaits.

42 gold-edged cards + 120-page full-colour guidebook packaged in a hardcover box. Gold-foil embellishments on top box and guidebook cover.
ISBN: 978-1-922573-85-8

More from Blue Angel Publishing

Oracle of Delphi

Prophecies From The Eternal Priestess

Suzy Cherub
Artwork by Briarly Collyns

Here, on the threshold of wisdom, you can commune with ancient seers, reclaim miracles and free the future. Here, your questions invite guidance, magic and activations. Here, you can experience a remembering that brings you home to the temple within. This exquisite oracle set is a portal to clarity and understanding. Shuffle the deck to invoke the eternal priestess, choose your cards and welcome wonder, healing visions and sacred empowerment.

44 cards and 176-page full-colour guidebook packaged in a hardcover box.
Navy-foil accents on top box and guidebook cover.
ISBN: 978-1-922573-75-9

More from Blue Angel Publishing®

Goddess Within Oracle

Healing with the Divine Feminine

Christabel Jessica
Artwork by Cecilia G.F. & Dannielle Jones

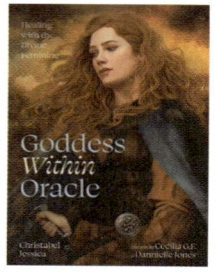

A barefoot maiden whispers of magic beneath the slender moon, a wizened crone prepares healing herbs in a woodland cottage, and elsewhere across time and place, an anointed priestess lights a candle to begin her temple ritual. The energy of the Goddess is with them all. Place your feet firmly on the earth, breathe into your bold and gracious heart, and feel her rise within you.

44 cards + 160-page full-color guidebook packaged in a hardcover box.
ISBN: 978-1-922573-79-7

More from Blue Angel Publishing®

Unveiling the Golden Age

A Visionary Tarot Experience

Izzy Ivy

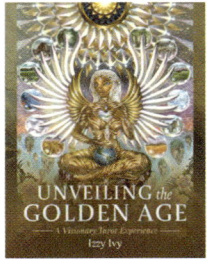

Traverse portals, glide down rainbows and feel the glory of your wings in this truly revelationary tarot and meditation deck. Intricate and intuitive, startling and reassuring, this 78-card offering was birthed from physical and multi-dimensional realms to ground and elevate the reader in a synergy of co-creative connection. Izzy Ivy's unique divinatory system offers insight, direction, healing practices and recalibration for yourself and others.

---

78 gold-edged cards and 304-page full-colour guidebook packaged in a hardcover box.
ISBN: 978-1-922573-74-2

For more information on this or
any Blue Angel Publishing® release,
please visit our website at:

www.blueangelonline.com